# Looking for Answers

Ron Benson

Lynn Bryan

Kim Newlove

Charolette Player

Liz Stenson

## CONSULTANTS

Susan Elliott

Diane Lomond

Ken MacInnis

Elizabeth Parchment

Prentice Hall Ginn Canada
Scarborough, Ontario

# Contents

   Selections with this symbol are available on audio.

   This symbol indicates student writing.

❦   Canadian selections are marked with this symbol.

# Moths and Moons

*Illustrated by Luc Melanson*

## Changes

*by Michael Spooner*

The earth sheds its winter quilts
and hurries on toward summer,
    as if it, too, is restless
    for the tree house and the bicycle.

The moon looks rounder
than it did last night;
    I think it knows that I am growing too.

The moth and butterfly emerge
from their cocoons, feeling
    how it feels when all your sleeves
    have grown too short again.

Each day my world shows
one more change;
    each day I see another one in me.

The earth rolls out of hibernation.
The moon slips through its phases in the sky.
The butterfly will try its wings today,

    and so will I,
    and so will I.

# The phase I'm going through

*by Michael Spooner*

I asked my mother
    why the moon is full sometimes
    and dark sometimes and sometimes in between.
She smiled a silly half-moon smile
    and said, "It's all
    a matter of which phase it's in."

I asked my father
    why the baby screams sometimes
    or laughs and wipes his supper in his hair.
He said that children go through phases.
    "Not to worry;
    he'll be through this in a year."

So if I turn my
    dark face to the world sometimes,
    or eat my hat with ketchup and with glue,
or yowl with cats when the moon is full,
    think nothing of it—
    it's just the phase I'm going through.

# The Marble Champ

*by Gary Soto*
*Illustrated by Scot Ritchie*

Lupe Medrano, a shy girl who spoke in whispers, was the school's spelling bee champion, winner of the reading contest at the public library three summers in a row, blue ribbon awardee in the science fair, the top student at her piano recital, and the playground grand champion in chess. She was a straight A student and—not counting kindergarten, when she had been stung by a wasp—never missed one day of elementary school. She had received a small trophy for this honor and had been congratulated by the mayor.

But though Lupe had a razor-sharp mind, she could not make her body, no matter how much she tried, run as fast as the other girls. She begged her body to move faster, but could never beat anyone in the fifty-metre dash.

The truth was that Lupe was no good in sports. She could not catch a pop-up or figure out in which direction to kick the soccer ball. One time she kicked the ball at her own goal and scored a point for the other team. She was no good at baseball or basketball either, and even had a hard time making a Hula-Hoop stay on her hips.

It wasn't until last year, when she was eleven years old, that she learned how to ride a bike. And even then she had to use training wheels. She could walk in the swimming pool but couldn't swim, and chanced roller-skating only when her father held her hand.

"I'll never be good at sports," she fumed one rainy day as she lay on her bed gazing at the shelf her father had made to hold her awards. "I wish I could win something, anything, even marbles."

At the word "marbles," she sat up. "That's it. Maybe I could be good at playing marbles." She hopped out of bed and rummaged through the closet until she found a can full of her brother's marbles. She poured the rich glass treasure on her bed and picked five of the most beautiful marbles.

She smoothed her bedspread and practised shooting, softly at first so that her aim would be accurate. The marble rolled from her thumb and clicked against the targeted marble. But the target wouldn't budge. She tried again and again. Her aim became accurate, but the power from her thumb made the marble move only a centimetre or two. Then she realized that the bedspread was slowing the marbles. She also had to admit that her thumb was weaker than the neck of a newborn chick.

She looked out the window. The rain was letting up, but the ground was too muddy to play. She sat cross-legged on the bed, rolling her five marbles between her palms. Yes, she thought, I could play marbles, and marbles is a sport. At that moment she realized that she had only two weeks to practise. The playground championship, the same one her brother had entered the previous year, was coming up. She had a lot to do.

To strengthen her wrists, she decided to do twenty pushups on her fingertips, five at a time. "One, two, three . . . ," she groaned. By the end of the first set she was breathing hard, and her muscles burned from exhaustion. She did one more set and decided that was enough push-ups for the first day. She squeezed a rubber eraser one hundred times, hoping it would strengthen her thumb. This seemed to work because the next day her thumb was sore. She could hardly hold a marble in her hand, let alone send it flying with

power. So Lupe rested that day and listened to her brother, who gave her tips on how to shoot: get low, aim with one eye, and place one knuckle on the ground.

"Think 'eye and thumb'—and let it rip!" he said.

After school the next day she left her homework in her backpack and practised three hours straight, taking time only to eat a candy bar for energy. With a Popsicle stick, she drew an odd-shaped circle and tossed in four marbles. She used her shooter, a milky agate with hypnotic swirls, to blast them. Her thumb *had* become stronger.

After practice, she squeezed the eraser for an hour. She ate dinner with her left hand to spare her shooting hand and said nothing to her parents about her dreams of athletic glory.

Practise, practise, practise. Squeeze, squeeze, squeeze. Lupe got better and beat her brother and Alfonso, a neighbor kid who was supposed to be a champ.

"Man, she's bad!" Alfonso said. "She can beat the other girls for sure. I think."

The weeks passed quickly. Lupe worked so hard that one day, while she was drying dishes, her mother asked why her thumb was swollen.

"It's muscle," Lupe explained. "I've been practising for the marbles championship."

"You, honey?" Her mother knew Lupe was no good at sports.

"Yeah. I beat Alfonso, and he's pretty good."

That night, over dinner, Mrs. Medrano said, "Honey, you should see Lupe's thumb."

"Huh?" Mr. Medrano said, wiping his mouth and looking at his daughter.

"Show your father."

"Do I have to?" an embarrassed Lupe asked.

"Go on, show your father."

Reluctantly, Lupe raised her hand and flexed her thumb. You could see the muscle.

The father put down his fork and asked, "What happened?"

"Dad, I've been working out. I've been squeezing an eraser."

"Why?"

"I'm going to enter the marbles championship."

Her father looked at her mother and then back at his daughter. "When is it, honey?"

"This Saturday. Can you come?"

The father had been planning to play racquetball with a friend Saturday, but he said he would be there. He knew his daughter thought she was no good at sports and he wanted to encourage her. He even rigged some lights in the backyard so she could practise after dark. He squatted with one knee on the ground, entranced by the sight of his daughter easily beating her brother.

The day of the championship began with a cold blustery sky. The sun was a silvery light behind slate clouds.

"I hope it clears up," her father said, rubbing his hands together as he returned from getting the newspaper. They ate breakfast, paced nervously around the house waiting for 10:00 to arrive, and walked the two blocks to the playground (though Mr. Medrano wanted to drive so Lupe wouldn't get tired). She signed up and was assigned her first match on baseball diamond number three.

Lupe, walking between her brother and her father, shook from the cold, not nerves. She took off her mittens, and everyone stared at her thumb. Someone asked, "How can you play with a broken thumb?" Lupe smiled and said nothing.

She beat her first opponent easily, and felt sorry for the girl because she didn't have anyone to cheer for her. Except for her sack of marbles, she was all alone. Lupe invited the girl, whose name was Rachel, to stay with them. She smiled and said, "O.K." The four of them walked to a card table in the middle of the outfield, where Lupe was assigned another opponent.

She also beat this girl, a fifth-grader named Yolanda, and asked her to join their group. They proceeded to more matches and more wins, and soon there was a crowd of people following Lupe to the finals to play a girl in a baseball cap. This girl seemed dead serious. She never even looked at Lupe.

"I don't know, Dad, she looks tough."

Rachel hugged Lupe and said, "Go get her."

"You can do it," her father encouraged. "Just think of the marbles, not the girl, and let your thumb do the work."

The other girl broke first and earned one marble. She missed her next shot, and Lupe, one eye closed, her thumb quivering with energy, blasted two marbles out of the circle but missed her next shot. Her opponent earned two more before

missing. She stamped her foot and said, "Shoot!" The score was three to two in favor of Miss Baseball Cap.

The referee stopped the game. "Back up, please, give them room," he shouted. Onlookers had gathered too tightly around the players.

Lupe then earned three marbles and was set to get her fourth when a gust of wind blew dust in her eyes and she missed badly. Her opponent quickly scored two marbles, tying the game, and moved ahead six to five on a lucky shot. Then she missed, and Lupe, whose eyes felt scratchy when she blinked, relied on instinct and thumb muscle to score the tying point. It was now six to six, with only three marbles left. Lupe blew her nose and studied the angles. She dropped to one knee, steadied her hand, and shot so hard she cracked two marbles from the circle. She was the winner!

"I did it!" Lupe said under her breath. She rose from her knees, which hurt from bending all day, and hugged her father. He hugged her back and smiled.

Everyone clapped, except Miss Baseball Cap, who made a face and stared at the ground. Lupe told her she was a great player, and they shook hands. A newspaper photographer took pictures of the two girls standing shoulder to shoulder, with Lupe holding the bigger trophy.

Lupe then played the winner of the boys' division, and after a poor start beat him eleven to four. She blasted the marbles, shattering one into sparkling slivers of glass. Her opponent looked on glumly as Lupe did what she did best—win!

The head referee and the president of the city's Marble Association stood with Lupe as she displayed her trophies for the newspaper photographer. Lupe shook hands with everyone, including a dog who had come over to see what the commotion was all about.

That night, the family went out

for pizza and set the two trophies on the table for everyone in the restaurant to see. People came up to congratulate Lupe, and she felt a little embarrassed, but her father said the trophies belonged there.

Back home, in the privacy of her bedroom, she placed the trophies on her shelf and was happy. She had always earned honors because of her brains, but winning in sports was a new experience. She thanked her tired thumb. "You did it, thumb. You made me champion." As its reward, Lupe went to the bathroom, filled the bathroom sink with warm water, and let her thumb swim and splash as it pleased. Then she climbed into bed and drifted into a hard-won sleep.

## ABOUT THE AUTHOR    GARY SOTO

Gary Soto was born and raised in Fresno, California. He attended the California State University in Fresno and the University of California. He is a prize-winnning poet, essayist, and children's book author. His poems have appeared in many literary magazines and in the *Norton Anthology of Modern Poetry*. He has also produced several short films. Gary lives with his family in Berkeley, California. He says, "I'm happy that the characters of my stories and poems are living in the hearts of young readers."

# Once Bitten

by David Hill

Illustrated by Peter Ferguson

The first time Cory got paid for his newspaper delivery round, he went to a coffee bar. It was up two flights of stairs, over a shoe shop on the town's busiest corner. He had been there once before with his mother.

It felt weird to be walking in by himself. The coffee bar was full of grownups, and they all seemed to be staring at him.

Cory pretended to be inspecting the food under its plastic covers. He found a fat triangle of fudge cake and slid it onto his tray. It looked a bit lonely by itself.

"Can I have a banana milk shake, please?" Cory asked the woman at the counter.

"Certainly, sir," the woman said. "Is sir by himself? Will sir be wanting anything else?"

She gave Cory a friendly grin, but he felt embarrassed. "I'll have one of those apricot granola bars, too, please," he said in as grown-up a voice as he could.

When Cory picked up his tray from the counter, the milk shake and the plate with the fudge cake started sliding around. He was trying to balance them, and hold the cellophane-wrapped granola bar, and stuff his change into his pockets, and look for a place to sit, all at the same time.

Cory headed for the one empty seat by the windows. He didn't dare look up till he got to the table and safely set the tray down. Then, for the first time, he saw the person on the opposite side.

It was a bikie*. Man! thought Cory, what a bikie! He was wearing a leather jacket and had long hair. He had a tattoo on the back of one hand that said DEATH RULES, and a tattoo on the other hand that said HI MOM. There was a dotted line tattooed across his forehead with LIFT TO INSPECT BRAIN tattooed above it.

The bikie's leather jacket had zips and chains and a studded dog collar hanging from it. He must sound like a heavy-metal rock band when he moves, Cory thought. One leg was sticking out from under the table, and Cory could see ripped black jeans above big black boots. Choice clothes! Cory thought. Hey, maybe the bikie had ridden his bike up the stairs into the coffee bar!

The bikie was drinking a cup of coffee and eating a cream doughnut. There was something else on his plate, too, but Cory didn't really notice it. He'd never been this close to a real live bikie before. He wondered if the guy would lean across the table and squash him into the sugar bowl or something.

*A "bikie" is the New Zealander term for biker.

12

The bikie didn't. He looked at Cory and gave him a "hiya" sort of nod.

Cory was just about to nod back when a voice began calling, "Sir? Excuse me sir, would you like a straw for your milk shake?" It was the woman at the counter.

Cory hurried over, feeling embarrassed again. "Thanks," he said. He took the straw and started back to his table.

Halfway there, Cory stopped and stared. No, it couldn't be happening! Yes, it was! The bikie had stopped eating his doughnut. He'd picked up Cory's apricot granola bar and had peeled off the cellophane wrapping. While Cory stood staring, the bikie took a thoughtful bite from one end.

For a second, Cory felt scared. Then he felt angry. That was *his* granola bar. He'd paid for it with *his* newspaper delivery money. He started moving forward again. By the time he reached the table, his mind was made up. He'd teach this bikie guy not to push paper carriers around.

Cory sat down at the table with his milk shake. He reached across and picked up the granola bar from the bikie's plate. He took a bite from it—from the end the bikie hadn't touched. Then he put it down on the plate again.

The bikie slowly raised his head and looked at Cory. He gave Cory another nod, picked up the granola bar, and took a second bite (a smaller and neater bite than Cory's) from his end. He put the bar down on his plate again.

Cory felt as though he were in one of those Wild West movies where the good guy and the bad guy stand facing each other along an empty street, waiting to see who draws first.

It was Cory who drew. He reached for the shrinking apricot granola bar again. He picked it up and, looking steadily at the tattooed terror sitting opposite him, he took another bite. Then he returned the bar to the bikie's plate.

Not much apricot in there, his taste buds were telling him. More like honey. You'd better try another coffee bar next payday.

The bikie gave Cory a third nod. He took up the remaining piece of granola bar. He held it between his thumb and forefinger and then bent his little finger like some polite person holding a nice cup of tea.

Very carefully, the bikie bit the final piece of bar exactly

in half. Then he lifted his eyebrows in a questioning sort of way. (Cory noticed that one eyebrow had a tiny tattoo above it that said UNZIP HERE.) He held the last little bar-bit across the table toward Cory.

Cory had no idea where his next words came from. He still felt as though he were in a movie.

"No, it's OK," Cory told the bikie. "You can have the rest of it. Tell you what—you can have these, too, if you're so hungry." Cory pushed his fudge cake and banana milk shake across the table. The bikie's mouth dropped open five centimetres.

"And in return—," Cory went on. He reached across, grabbed the bikie's cream doughnut, and took the biggest bite he could. The bikie's mouth dropped open ten centimetres.

Cory stood up, bits of doughnut cream sticking to his chin, and walked as calmly as he could out of the coffee bar. He half expected people to start cheering. He also half expected a motorbike to start up and come roaring through the tables and down the stairs after him.

At the bus stop a few minutes later, Cory could hardly believe what he'd done. His legs were shaking, and his heart was bumping. But he felt great. He hadn't eaten any of the other things he'd paid for, but he'd won, all right. He'd really given that bikie something to chew on.

Paper Carriers 1, Bikies 0, Cory thought, and started laughing. The other people waiting for the bus looked at him in surprise.

As the bus arrived, Cory reached for the change he'd stuffed into his pocket after buying his things in the coffee bar. His fingers closed on the cool metal coins. They closed on something else as well. Something thin and light and crackly.

What's this? Cory wondered. He pulled the something out of his pocket. There in his hand, still inside its cellophane wrapper, lay his own, untouched, apricot granola bar.

## ABOUT THE AUTHOR  DAVID HILL

David Hill lives in New Plymouth, on the west coast of New Zealand's North Island. He has been a high school teacher, a soldier, and a van driver. He has written plays and novels for teenagers and younger readers. His novels *See Ya Simon* and *Take It Easy* have both been published in the United States. He wrote "Once Bitten" because he wanted to put his biker friend, Mike, in a story. David is married with two grown-up children. He likes reading, hiking, astronomy, and cheering for New Zealand's rugby football team.

# Tub Under the Stars

*by Yoshiko Uchida*
*Illustrated by Don Kilby*

*Yoshiko Uchida's memories of growing up in the 1930s were part of the invisible thread that linked her to her heritage...*

Papa was a terrible driver. He had taught himself how to drive, and nobody had ever told him to look in both directions before driving through an intersection. Usually, he looked one way, and if nothing was coming, he sailed right through with his usual buoyant confidence.

One Sunday afternoon, after we'd taken a friend of Mama's for a drive, Papa made that mistake once too often. Just two blocks from home, Papa came to a corner, looked to the left, and kept going. Unfortunately, another car was coming from the right. And that's when it happened.

We were hit broadside, and our bulky Buick simply toppled over and lay on its side like a beached whale.

Drowsing in the backseat, I was suddenly jolted on top of Mama and proceeded to scream at the top of my lungs. Papa somehow managed to get through the window and pulled the rest of us out.

"Are you all right?" he asked each of us.

"Yes, Papa," we answered feebly. And we emerged one by one,

to the astonishment of the onlookers who, having heard my screams, probably expected me at least to have a broken arm or leg.

Fortunately, we suffered only minor bumps, cuts, and bruises, and although a bit wobbly, we were able to walk home.

For me the accident was a major event worthy of an illustrated page in my diary, but Papa brushed it aside as a minor inconvenience and kept right on driving as he always had.

One summer he drove us to Livingston to visit Mr. and Mrs. Okubo. They were among the early Japanese families who had settled there, tamed the dry windblown earth, and coaxed grapes to flourish where nothing had grown before. I could hardly wait to spend a few days on a real farm, for I was a child of the city who walked on sidewalks and knew only dogs and cats.

Mama was always nervous about Papa's driving, but after the accident, she was even more so. She usually sat in the back with me, often reaching out to grab my arm whenever Papa went too fast or got too close to a streetcar.

"Be careful, Papa San," she would call out. "You're going too fast." But I don't think Papa ever listened.

Keiko usually sat in front with him because she wanted to watch his every move. Already she had a fairly good idea of how to drive and was dying to get behind the wheel. In a weak moment, Papa had said that maybe she could when we got out into the countryside.

As we turned off the main highway, it seemed as though we were driving through a vast ocean of vineyards that spread out on both sides of the dusty road. Before long we could see the Okubo water pump windmill sprouting up among the grapevines.

"There it is!" Keiko shouted. "There's the Okubo farm!"

She reminded Papa of his earlier promise and convinced him there was nothing on the deserted road that she could possibly hit. Papa knew he would never hear the end of it if he didn't give her a chance, so he stopped the car.

Keiko was in heaven as Papa let her slide over behind the wheel. But poor Mama was clutching my arm again.

"Careful, Kei Chan," she cautioned. "Be careful."

Keiko started slowly, like a tired turtle. But by the time she made the final turn toward the farm, she was feeling confident and picking up a little speed.

"Honk the horn to let them know we're here," Papa said.

At which point Keiko not only honked the horn, but simultaneously crashed into Jick's dog house, knocked it over on its side, and stopped just inches short of the walnut tree.

"Look out, for heaven's sake," we all shouted. "Look out!"

Jick barked furiously at the sudden assault on his territory, and the chickens scrambled in every direction, screeching and cackling as though the end of the world had come.

The startled Okubos rushed from their house, blinking in the sun, surveying with alarm what only moments before had been their peaceful yard.

"We're here!" Keiko shouted, as if they needed to be told. "We're here!"

Because the Okubos' two grown daughters had already left home, they welcomed my sister and me as though we were their grandchildren, and we called them Oji San (uncle) and Oba San (auntie).

Oji San gave us a quick tour of the farm. He showed us how to pump water from the well and put our heads down to gulp the cold water that came gushing out. He pointed to the outhouse, saying, "I guess you've never used one of those before." We certainly hadn't. Whenever I had to use it, I held my breath and got out as fast as I could.

He also let us look for eggs in the henhouse, and took us to the barn where we staggered about in the hayloft, trying to pitch hay with forks that were bigger than we were.

He saved the best for last, taking us to a fenced enclosure where two dusty mules ambled over to greet us.

"Meet Tom and Jerry," he said. Then pulling some scraggly weeds by the fence, he told us to feed them to the mules.

I thrust some weeds at them and the mules grabbed them hungrily, showing their enormous yellow teeth. They seemed friendly enough, but I was rather glad they were on the other side of the fence.

"They like you," Oji San said. "Maybe they'll do something nice for you later on."

"Like what, Oji San?"

Oji San just grinned and smashed his felt hat down over his forehead. "You'll see," he said. "Wait and see."

Sitting on mats spread out under the walnut tree, we had a wonderful picnic supper of soy-drenched chicken and corn grilled over an outdoor pit. There were rice balls, too, sprinkled with black sesame seeds that looked like tiny ants.

Oji San waited until the sun had dipped down behind the dusty grapevines and a soft dusky haze settled in the air. Then he announced he was taking us all on a moonlight ride through the vineyards. It was more than we'd ever hoped for.

Keiko took her usual place up front by Oji San, hoping for a brief chance at the reins. Mama and Papa chatted quietly with Oba San, and I lay stretched out in the back, looking up at the enormous night sky.

19

There seemed to be millions and billions of stars up there. More than I'd ever imagined existed in the universe. They seemed brighter and closer than they were in Berkeley. It was as though the entire sky had dropped closer to Earth to spread out its full glory right there in front of me.

I listened to the slow *clop-clop* of the mules as they plodded through the fields, probably wondering why they were pulling a wagonload of people in the dark, instead of hauling boxes of grapes to the shed under the hot, dry sun.

I could hear crickets singing and frogs croaking and all the other gentle night sounds of the country. I felt as though I were in another more immense, never-ending world, and wished I could keep riding forever to the ends of the earth.

When we got back to the farm, it was time for an outdoor Japanese bath. Oji San built a fire under a square tin tub filled with water, banking the fire when the water was hot and inserting a wooden float so we wouldn't burn our feet or backsides when we got in.

Oba San hung some sheets on ropes strung around the tub and called out, "*Sah, ofuro*! Come, Kei Chan, Yo Chan. The bath is ready. You girls go first."

Mama gave us careful instructions about proper bathing procedures. "Wash and rinse yourselves outside before you get into the tub," she reminded us. "And keep the water clean."

When we were ready to climb in, I saw steam rising from the water and was afraid I'd be boiled alive. "You go first," I told my sister.

As always, Keiko was fearless. She jumped right in and sank down in the steaming water up to her neck.

"Ooooooh, this feels wonderful!" she said.

I quickly squeezed in next to her, and we let the warm water gurgle up to our chins.

Keiko looked up at the glorious night sky and sighed, "I could stay here forever."

"Where? In the tub?"

"No, silly. In Livingston, of course."

Long after I came home, I remembered Livingston, not as the small dusty farm it was, but as a magical place.

Even now, when I close my eyes, I can see the smiling, sun-browned faces of Oji San and Oba San welcoming us to their farm. I can hear our watery giggles in the steaming outdoor tub, and I can hear the small quiet songs of the creatures in the fields.

But most of all I remember the wagon ride and see again that night sky exploding with stars. It is like a beautiful speckled stone I can take from the pocket of my memory to look at over and over, remembering again the sweet peace of that little farm.

I have written about it in several of my books and stories, and the memory of it even now brings a rush of joy to my heart.

## ABOUT THE AUTHOR   YOSHIKO UCHIDA

Yoshiko Uchida was born in 1921 in Alameda, California. She began her career as a teacher while interned for a year in a Japanese relocation camp during World War II. She was released from the camp to pursue her education on the East Coast. After teaching for a few more years, she decided to work as a secretary in order to find more time to write. Eventually, her success allowed her to become a full-time writer. Yoshiko became the author of over thirty books and dozens of short stories for children. Most of her stories were about the experiences of Japanese children in the United States or Japan. Yoshiko received many honors and awards for her work. She died in 1992 in Berkeley, California.

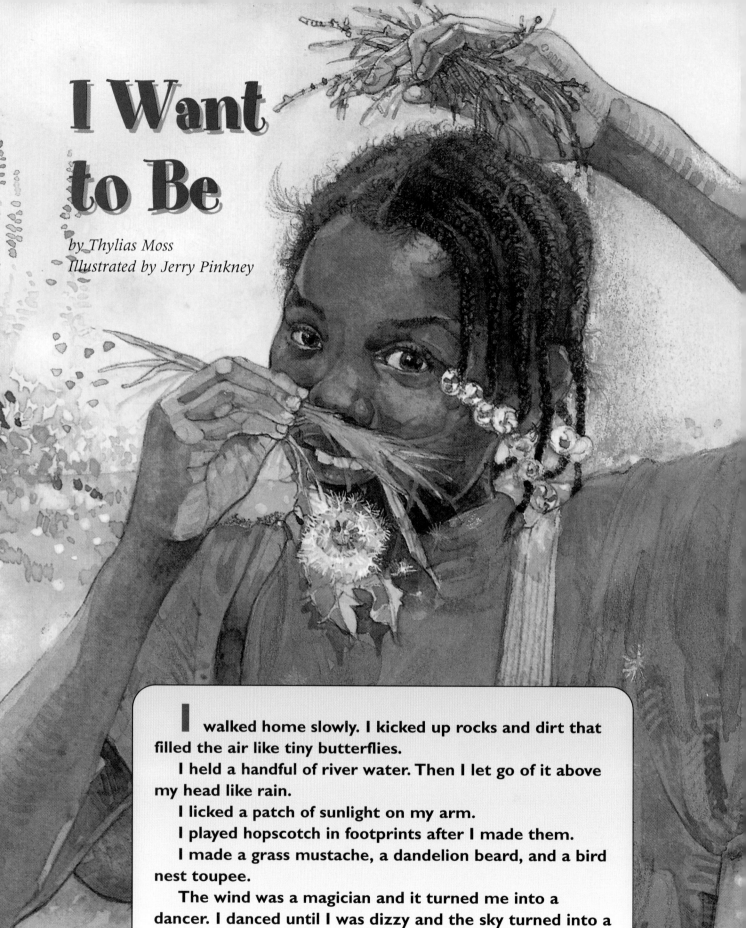

# I Want to Be

by Thylias Moss
Illustrated by Jerry Pinkney

I walked home slowly. I kicked up rocks and dirt that filled the air like tiny butterflies.

I held a handful of river water. Then I let go of it above my head like rain.

I licked a patch of sunlight on my arm.

I played hopscotch in footprints after I made them.

I made a grass mustache, a dandelion beard, and a bird nest toupee.

The wind was a magician and it turned me into a dancer. I danced until I was dizzy and the sky turned into a lake so I stood on my head and was a fish swimming in it.

I double-dutched with strands of rainbow. Then I fastened the strands to my hair and my toes and became a fiddle that sunbeams played. Then I sang with the oxygen choir.

At sunset I was a firefighter and I squirted water at the sun until it turned into the moon and until it was so dark the stars couldn't play hide-and-seek anymore.

"All home free," I said.

By the time I got home, I knew what I wanted to be.

I want to be big but not so big that a mountain or a mosque or a synagogue seems small.

I want to be strong but not so strong that a kite seems weak.

I want to be old but not so old that Mars and Jupiter and redwoods seem young.

I want to be fast but not so fast that lightning seems slow.

I want to be wise but not so wise that I can't learn anything.

I want to be beautiful but not so beautiful that a train moving in the sun like a metal peacock's flowing feathers on tracks that are like stilts a thousand kilometres long laid down like a ladder up a flat mountain (wow!) seems dull.

I want to be green but not so green that I can't also be purple.

I want to be tall but not so tall that nothing is above me. Up must still be somewhere, with clouds and sky.

I want to be quiet but not so quiet that nobody can hear me. I also want to be sound, a whole orchestra with two bassoons and an army of cellos.

Sometimes I want to be just the triangle, a tinkle that sounds like an itch.

I want to be still but not so still that I turn into a mannequin or get mistaken for a tree.

I want to be in motion but I want the ants in my pants to sometimes take a vacation.

Sometimes I want to be slow but not so slow that everything passes me by.

Sometimes I want to be small but not so small that I am easy to miss. About the size of the thought of a bud before it opens and becomes a universe in which bees orbit like planets.

Sometimes I want to be invisible but not gone.

Sometimes I want to be weightless and floating on air, able to fly when I want to and able to stay on the ground when I feel like it. I want to be a leaf that is part canoe riding the water as if it's a liquid horse. I want to be comfortable in all the elements.

I want to be a language, a way to share thoughts. What my grandmother says when she speaks in tongues. That's also music. I want to be my other grandmother's hands, when she signs, when she seems to be blessing everything.

I want to be all the people I know, then I want

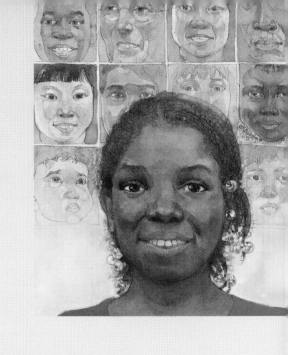

to know more people so I can be them too. Then they can all be me. I want to be a new kind of earthquake, rocking the world as if it's a baby in a cradle.

I want to be eyes looking, looking everywhere.
I want to be ears hearing, hearing everything.
I want to be hands touching, touching everything.
I want to be mouth tasting, tasting everything.
I want to be heart feeling, feeling everything.
I want to be life doing, doing everything.

That's all.

## ABOUT THE AUTHOR   THYLIAS MOSS

Born in Cleveland, Ohio, Thylias Moss has been writing since she was six years old. Her first published poem appeared in her church bulletin when she was seven. As she once said, "The only thing I was before I was a writer was a female." Today she is the award-winning author of several volumes of poetry and a soon to be published autobiography. *I Want to Be* is her first children's book. Her second children's book *Somewhere Else Right Now* will be published in 1998. Thylias lives in Ann Arbor, Michigan.

# Dreams, Hopes, and Challenges

*as told to Lynn Bryan*

*Imagine leaving everything you know behind and starting all over again in a new country. That's what students in Ms. Leahy's English as a Second Language (ESL) class have had to do. Scary? Yes! Yet out of this challenge have come new and exciting hopes and dreams—and the courage to work toward making them come true.*

Ms. Leahy's ESL class

## Navdeep

Up until just one and a half years ago, Navdeep Singh Sohal lived in India with his parents. Then his uncle, who was living in Canada, came over to India to visit. He got to know Navdeep and saw great potential in him. He asked Navdeep's father if he would let his son come to Canada to live with him as his adopted son. Navdeep's father agreed, but he told Navdeep that the final decision would be left up to him.

Navdeep chose to go. Although it was difficult to leave his family and friends in India, he was excited about starting a new life in Canada. Soon he was involved in all sorts of new things—tobogganing, skating, basketball, and volleyball. Then members of an Indo Canadian rock band heard Navdeep sing a solo at a wedding and asked him to join their group. He now sings with them at parties, weddings, and in local concerts. He has even been invited to sing with a Vancouver band and make a tape!

Being in a band is one of Navdeep's dreams, but he's also aiming to win scholarships that will take him to university. There he wants to study to become a doctor. Whatever he does, he's bound to do well, for his motto is "I want to be the best!"

## Anh

Eleven-year-old Anh Ngo used to live in Vietnam. Her country had been devastated by a war and life was very difficult. Anh's parents felt their children would have a chance for a better life in another country, so they decided to escape. It wasn't easy—the boat they fled on was chased and attacked, and they were out of food and water for days. At last, Anh, her brother, and their father were among those rescued and taken to a refugee camp in the Philippines. After many months of waiting, Anh's father received news that his family would soon leave for Canada.

Once in Canada everything seemed strange and overwhelming to Anh— the cold and snow of a Canadian winter, the language, the clothes, the food, the stores, and her new school. Deep inside, however, she knew she could meet the challenge of these new things. After all, hadn't she managed to escape Vietnam and get through being in the refugee camp?

Going to school is the highlight of Anh's new life. She feels safe and welcome there, and is proud of how well she has learned English. She is able to act as a translator for Phuong, a new Vietnamese student in her class.

Anh hopes to become an ESL teacher, and she has another very special dream too. She loves to read stories and draw pictures to go with them—perhaps someday Anh will be a famous illustrator of children's books!

# Danny

Just eight months ago, Danny Gruner immigrated to Canada from Germany. She and Anh became best friends right away, despite their differences in language and life experiences. At first they just exchanged smiles and played games together, but as Danny learned to speak English, she and Anh could talk about things and giggle over funny situations. Danny learned English quickly for she found similarities in many English and German words. Besides, she had taken a little English at school in Germany.

When Danny's parents first talked with her and her brother about moving to the Okanagan Valley in Canada, Danny felt quite confused. She was excited about the opportunities her parents described, but when she thought about the things she'd leave behind, she felt saddened too. There was her favorite horse, Esther, her friends, her class at school, and her grandparents.

"Sometimes it's still really hard for me," Danny says. "Sometimes I just have to sit down and cry about all the things I miss." However, these moments of emptiness are balanced by the kind and friendly people she has met and the thrill of new experiences. Not long after Danny's family arrived, a neighbor on the property next door let Danny lead one of their miniature ponies around the ring at the Armstrong Fair. Danny was delighted! She can hardly wait until she gets a pony of her own. She is amazed at all the open countryside in Canada. "It feels like you could just jump on a horse and ride anywhere!" Danny says. Horses are a part of her dream for her future: she hopes to go to the Olympics and compete in dressage riding.

Today, Danny is proud of herself for saying "Yes" to the challenge of leaving Germany. "I think we all made a really, really good choice!" she says.

# Nathan

Nathan Meier clearly recalls the day his father announced that their family was moving to Canada. They lived in Switzerland, and although it was a wonderful place to be, the cost of living was high. It took a lot of money to feed a family of eight boys and one girl. To support his family, Nathan's father had to teach music from 5:00 a.m. to 11:00 p.m. and work as a butcher too. It wouldn't be that way in Canada, so they'd get to see more of him.

Nathan found that part exciting, but he wasn't sure he wanted to leave Switzerland or his friends. He says that the countryside where he lived was very beautiful, and his friends all lived close by. They could swim, fish, and play soccer together. In the winter, they skied in the nearby mountains.

"When I left, I wanted to bring Switzerland with me," Nathan says wistfully. Imagine his delight when he discovered that his new home in Canada had much of what he had left behind: snow, mountains, fields, fruit trees, lakes—and more! He could ski in the winter and swim and play soccer in the summer, just as he had always done.

Nathan had come from a school of fifty students, with only seven in his class. His new school had over four hundred students! Luckily, his ESL class was small so that helped a bit. As well, Nathan could turn to Danny for help in translating, for he had learned to speak German in school, which meant they had that language in common.

Nathan soon found new friends, and began making a name for himself in the school. Although English was very new to him, he scored a B in math in just one month. At the school Remembrance Day service he shared his musical talents by playing "Taps" on his trumpet. Nathan really excels in soccer too. He hopes to develop his skill even further and someday play on Canada's national soccer team.

Now that he's made the move to Canada and feels more comfortable, Nathan comments, "I like Switzerland. I like Canada—maybe even Canada is better."

## Ekaterina

In June of this year, Ekaterina Brovina and her family emigrated from Siberia in the northern part of Russia. Her father had worked in Canada at one time and, liking the country very much, he decided to move his family here.

The Brovin family flew to Montreal where they spent the summer enjoying the beauty of the city and many new experiences. Then they started on a trip across Canada, headed for Vernon, B.C. During their five-day drive, they became aware that Canada, like Russia, is an expansive country with a wide range of landscapes, towns, and cities. Ekaterina was delighted with everything Canadian from the majestic Niagara Falls to the year-round swimming pool and hot tub at the Recreation Centre in Vernon.

Although Ekaterina is happy and comfortable in her new home, a move is never easy. There are times of loneliness when she thinks about her friends and relatives in Russia. She really misses them and her big dog, Max. Learning a new language is difficult as well; however, Ekaterina has persevered and is steadily becoming more familiar with English.

Large supermarkets, big houses, and Canadian names are all rather intriguing to Ekaterina. She has chosen to be called Katy, a Canadian name, which translated into Russian would be Katya. Katy is not sure what her dreams are for her own future, but she does have a dream that one day her relatives and friends will come to Canada and live with her.

## Changes

When I was 4, I thought that I would always like to play with my lego and transformers. I also was positive that girls had germs and that they were highly contagious. But now, 9 years later, I look back to see how much I have changed. I no longer spend hours on end playing lego, transformers, and the like, and girls no longer have a deadly disease. Brussels sprouts, tomatoes, and lima beans are no longer poison. When I look at my kindergarten pictures, I cannot find myself, and when I finally do, I'm shocked. When I look back, I'm surprised at what I see, but I'm sure someday I'll look back to when I was 13 and see how much I've changed since then. Change is neither good nor bad, but it is inevitable. You probably will not notice that you are changing unless you actually think about it. Change is uncontrollable because no matter what, you will age and you will mature physically and mentally.

— Ted Torbicki, Grade 7

> When I get a writing assignment, I often cannot come up with any ideas at first. So, I usually think about it in my spare time. I enjoy writing assignments with set topics.

Ted Torbicki

## Dear Diary

Today the teacher asked the class what we would hope to be doing in 20 years. The question really stunned me because no one has ever asked me that question.

I had to think about it for a while because I'd never thought about that question before. I've always had other things on my mind which were going on at that present time. After thinking long and hard about what she said, I told my teacher that in 20 years I hoped to be a successful lawyer, and to be happily married to a great man. I also hope to have two or three kids and live in a huge grey brick house. I just hope that one day I will be able to face my challenge and to live up to my dream.

–Leanne Gomes, Grade 7

## I'd Like to Be

I'd like to be a doctor
Oh, no I'm not that smart.
I'd like to be an artist
But I can't make works of art.
I'd like to be an actress
But I wouldn't get the part.
I'd like to be Santa Claus
But I don't have that much heart.
I'd like to be a dentist
Oh, no I'm not that steady.
I'd like to be a mountain climber
But what if there's a Yeti?
I'd like to be a shoe shiner
But that job seems too petty.
I'd like to be myself
For that I think I'm ready.

— Kathryn Maslanka, Age 12

## When I'm 12

Soon I will be 12 years old and in grade seven. I will be able to try out for the volleyball and basketball teams. I am hoping to make at least one of them and I have been practising both sports. It seems like the grade sevens get so many more opportunities than the junior grades do. I will be old enough to babysit, too. I have younger neighbors and baby cousins who I can babysit. My brother will be in high school, and he won't be able to walk the Kindergartens to school anymore. I will not mind taking over that job. All these good things seem so far away, but I really won't have to wait long at all!

— Kaitlin O'Leary, Grade 6

## Children's Dreams

Many children have different dreams. I, in particular, have a dream to one day be an entertainer. I sometimes dream about being the best entertainer in the world just like Michael Jackson, but better. I dream that millions of crazed fans chant my name. I would dress in baggy jeans and a very baggy white T-shirt. Most people think that you have to be a good singer when you're small, but I don't. I will one day be an entertainer and show all those people that thought I couldn't do it. Then we will see who's laughing. I can't wait till I grow up.

—Justin Dumont, Age 13

# I Have a Dream

I have a dream that I would like to be a veterinarian. I would like to graduate from University and then have my own veterinary clinic. I would love to help animals of all kinds. I would like to help save animals from being abused or used for gambling.

I would do whatever it takes to make sure that animals are not used in any so called "sport" where one animal dies or is hurt.

I have a dream about saving animals of all kinds from abuse and I hope to find cures for diseases animals can get or have. I want to be famous for my work in animal research and abuse against animals. I have a dream.

—Natalie Lind, Age 13

Making up stories is like a second nature to me. With anything I do, whether it's brushing my teeth or riding my bike, I think of it in story form. I hope that I'll always go on composing stories.

Caitlin Kopperson

## The Search For Recognition

I took a deep breath and placed my letter into the mailbox. My story would soon be on its way to the publishers! I wanted to make an impression on the world; I wanted to say, "Hey! Look at me! I have ideas to share with you." It was like a search. A search to discover my true calling, the way I could make the world better or at least wiser. To become an author was my dream, but I knew that the only way my dream would come true was through hard work and problems. Every kid goes on this search, even if not every kid finds what they're looking for. After I mailed my story, I paced the house for days. When an answer finally came, I was too nervous to open the envelope for almost a week. I did open it, though. Inside was a polite letter explaining that they could not use my story. I'm not giving up, though! Wish me and every other kid luck in our searches!

– Caitlin Kopperson, Age 11

# Winter Camp Out

*by Vera Jensen*
*Illustrated by John Mantha*

"Sleep in the snow? You're joking."

Kamloops, British Columbia, is on the other side of the world from Brisbane, Australia, and I knew I had a lot to learn about Canadian winters. But sleep in the snow? I didn't believe it.

"Bet Aussie, here, is too soft to come along," Barry said.

"You're on, mate," I said.

Dad sort of raised his eyebrows at the length of the equipment list, but he signed the permission slip.

"At least you won't have to worry about snakes," he said.

It was a couple of weeks later. Stan, the first bloke I'd met in Canada who understood 'stralian, had been coaching me on the use of snow shoes, the one piece of equipment provided by the school. We were in the basement checking out the rest of the stuff Mom and Dad had either bought or borrowed for me.

"Want to come over to Barry's place?" Stan asked. "He thinks he's so tough he knows more about winter camping than anyone. Says he never reads the equipment list. Maybe you can help me talk some sense into him."

"Not me, mate. Barry thinks I'm whacko, and isn't shy about letting me know it. I don't need the aggravation."

"No prob. Don't forget extra socks," Stan warned me again.

Mom took him dead serious and pushed two more pairs into my pack.

It was early the next Saturday and still dark out when I woke. This was the weekend I was going to find out if an Aussie could make it in the snow. There were a few white flakes floating in the air when Stan and his Dad picked me up. His Mom was along too. She'd take the truck back and pick us up again late Sunday afternoon. The 4 by 4 bucked and skidded, but made it safely up the steep track to the bottom of the mountain trail.

Stan's Dad unloaded a snowmobile and a sled from the back of the truck.

Other trucks arrived and left again, leaving eight guys, four girls, another Dad, someone's mother, and Mr. Bowman, our teacher, stomping around in the snow.

Stan and Mr. Bowman showed me how to lash the sleeping bags and some of the heavier equipment to the sled, which was hitched to the snowmobile.

Stan's Dad disappeared up the mountain trail on the snowmobile. We picked up our back packs, strapped on our snowshoes, and followed. The sled had left a flattened trail but the snow was deep and soft on either side.

"Should be about two and a half maybe three metres of snow up at the campsite," Mr. Bowman told me. "Perfect for snow caves."

"Yes, sir," I agreed, but I still secretly believed that this was some kind of a joke and that there would be cabins waiting for us.

Stan had taken me out every night for the past week to practise snowshoeing, but tramping up and down the hills behind his house was not like this endless twisting trail that wound up the side of the mountain. My legs ached, my feet were numb, and my back pack felt like it weighed a tonne by the time we stopped for lunch.

"Check your feet," advised Stan as I pulled out the lunch Mom had packed for me.

Stan's Dad had prepared hot chocolate for us over a couple of small burners. I followed Stan's advice, collected my mug of chocolate, and was digging out one of Mom's sandwiches when I noticed Barry sitting on the edge of the sled.

"You look right crook, mate," I said as I joined him.

"Butt out, Aussie, you don't know from nothing."

I backed off.

Stan joined me. "Barry forgot his lunch, have you got anything extra?"

My Mom always packs extra. I handed over a sandwich and some cookies. Stan had extra too.

"Butt out, Stan," Barry muttered, "I don't need your Aussie handouts."

"Eat 'em, or you'll really wimp out," yelled Stan. "You want to get hypothermia?"

"OK, OK," Barry took the food.

It was too cold to stand around so we were soon headed up the trail again. We stopped once or twice for a handful of trail mix, but I was hungry and tired when I saw Stan's Dad and the snowmobile had stopped again in a large clearing. There was not a cabin in sight.

Mr. Bowman broke us up into small groups.

"Stan, you, Luke, and Barry build your cave over there." He pointed to a white drift on the edge of the clearing.

We started digging. Stan made us take our time, and when Barry got careless and tried to rush, he managed to send him off to help one of the other fathers to build the latrines.

At last our cave was dug out to Stan's satisfaction. A narrow tunnel led down and then up. The cave was just wide enough for three sleeping bags and high enough for us to sit up.

Mr. Bowman called me to help collect firewood. He showed me how to find dead branches under the trees and even pulled some down from the trees themselves.

Suddenly, as he was chopping at a dead branch, Mr. Bowman disappeared in a cloud of fluffy snow. I floundered over to help but, snowshoes and all, I slid down on top of him.

We were in a hole under the tree but caught up by the branches less than a metre from the ground. Every movement brought more snow down on top of us. We hung onto the branches over our heads and tried to balance on the slippery branches.

My snowshoes slipped off.

"No problem," Mr. Bowman assured me, "mine are gone too. If a porcupine doesn't get them, we'll find them next summer. Now, yell, we need some help here."

More snow tumbled down as we yelled.

"Hey, Aussie, where are you?" It was Barry's voice.

"Down here," I shouted.

"Trying to get back down under, eh?" Barry laughed. "Hang on, I'll get a rope."

My arms were aching before Barry got back with the rope, and I was starting to shiver.

"Got to get the Aussie out," we heard him shout. "He was trying to take a short cut home."

"Over here, Barry," Mr. Bowman called out, "on your stomach. Spread your weight, and don't come too close."

A rope slipped over the edge of the snow.

Mr. Bowman caught it with one hand and looped it around my waist.

"Hang onto the rope," he told me, "and try not to kick me in the face."

"Yes, sir."

"Haul away, Barry."

The rope caught under my armpits. I dug in with my feet and struggled up.

"Untie the rope and throw it to Bowman," Barry shouted, "then crawl over here, on your belly, man, on your belly."

I did as he said. Stan was there, too, with the end of the rope tied around his body like the anchor man for a tug-of-war.

"Grab on," he said. "Mr. Bowman is going to be a lot heavier than you were."

"Pull away," Mr. Bowman's voice was muffled by the snow.

We pulled.

"Well done, boys." Mr. Bowman struggled to his feet slapping at the snow clinging to his parka. "Stan, help us get this snow out of our clothes, Barry's too."

We pulled off our parkas and shook away the snow, and then brushed the caked stuff out of the tops of our boots.

"Change into dry socks as soon as we get back," advised Mr. Bowman as we hitched the dead wood we'd gathered into a bundle with Barry's rope and pulled it behind us. Barry and Stan went ahead, flattening a trail for us with their snowshoes.

There was a fire burning back at the campsite. I noticed Barry take off his snowshoes and boots and hold his feet as close to the fire as possible while I dug in my pack for dry socks.

Groups of kids and grownups were cooking supper. Stan's Dad had a pot of beans bubbling. I added the cut-up weiners I'd brought along. While we ate that, Stan melted some snow and cooked up dried vegetable noodles and Hamburger Helper. We ate it all. Then I pulled out the chocolate peanut butter bars my Mom makes.

The hot food took away the last of my shivers. I wasn't exactly warm but I wasn't quite so cold either.

I began to notice that Barry had moved away from the rest of us, closer to the fire. He'd eaten a plate full of beans and weiners and he was munching on Mom's goodies all right but he could barely walk.

There was a pinched blue look to his face. He was trying to keep close to the fire but he was avoiding Mr. Bowman and the other adults at the same time.

Aussies don't like snitches, but I thought somebody should be checking Barry out.

The grownups were standing together on the far side of the fire but they moved like lightning when I told them what I'd noticed.

Barry was hustled over to the sled. Someone pulled off his boots and socks. Someone shouted for Stan and me.

There was nothing in Barry's pack except an extra sweater, a towel, a Swiss hunting knife, his camping set of pans and utensils, and three more tins of beans.

Stan's Mom, like mine, believed in extras. In a very short time, Barry was re-dressed from the skin out, from spare boots to an extra down jacket under the borrowed parka.

He was still limping when he came back to the campfire where we were drinking more hot chocolate.

He punched me on the shoulder. "You told them, didn't you, Aussie?"

"Had to, mate, you were crook."

He looked puzzled for a moment, then he grinned.

"Guess I was about crook as I could get," he punched my shoulder again.

"Thanks," he said, "mate."

"Good on ya, Barry," laughed Stan in his best 'stralian, "Good on ya, mate."

## ABOUT THE AUTHOR  VERA JENSEN

Vera Jensen was born and raised on Vancouver Island. She left home at seventeen to study journalism at the University of Washington in Seattle. Her first writing experience was reporting current events for a local newspaper. Later, she began a new career as a teacher. After twenty years of writing report cards, lesson plans, and letters to parents, Vera retired to the beach at Comox, British Columbia, where she still gardens and writes.

# Problem Solvers

*as told to Catherine Rondina*

**M**y name is Sunil Patel and I am a Grade 6 student at Rosewell Avenue Public School. Recently, I, an ordinary, mild-mannered student, came up with a plan to solve some of the problems at my school. Well, actually, my teacher came up with the plan, but my friends and I helped.

Rosewell Avenue is a pretty average school and we have lots of good times there. But like most schools, every once in a while there's trouble. For instance, I remember last spring when we had this basketball contest. Boy, did it cause a lot of trouble!

The contest was pretty straight-forward. The students were divided into equal teams and the team who scored the most baskets would be the winner. We had two weeks to practise for the big day. Everything seemed to be going fine until Pui-Ying Chiu started bragging that her team was doing better at shooting hoops than my team. Just between you and me, she had a great shot, but still, how could she say that her team was better?

One recess, as Pui-Ying was practising in the schoolyard, I decided to show her just who ruled the basketball court. So I went up to her and asked her if she wanted to see a real pro in action. She laughed and wouldn't hand over the ball. I kept asking her to let me take a shot and soon there was a crowd of kids gathered around us. Before we knew it, her friends were chanting for her and my friends were cheering for me. Pui-Ying and I started to tug on

the ball. Neither of us wanted to let the other get a shot away. Suddenly, half the Grade 6 class was pushing and shoving each other.

Unfortunately, Ms. Lee, our homeroom teacher, was on yard duty and saw this big commotion. She came over to see what was going on. She blew her whistle, which meant we all had to return to our classroom immediately. We were caught red-handed; we were toast. All we could do was wait for our punishment to be decided. When Principal MacKay showed up at our classroom, I knew we had to think of something, and fast.

"Now students" she said, "you know the situation got out of hand. What are we going to do about that?"

The room was totally silent as we all stared at our feet.

"Tell you what we're going to do," said Principal MacKay. "Ms. Lee and I have discussed this and we've decided to let you kids come up with your own solution. Why don't you all take a little time to think about it?" she added with a smile, " and tomorrow morning I want to see a written report from this group on how to prevent this type of trouble from happening again at Rosewell Avenue."

"That's it?" I said, before I even realized I had spoken aloud.

"That's it," said Principal MacKay. "And, Sunil, you can present the report to me in my office tomorrow."

Me and my big mouth!

That afternoon, Ms. Lee said she would let us spend some time on our assignment for Principal MacKay. But first we had to work on our Social Studies unit. "Today, boys and girls," she said, "we are going to discuss a program that is being run at another school. The program is called Problem Solvers, and the students in that school have learned to solve problems for themselves." She grinned and the whole class let out a cheer. Now we'd know where to start on our report for the principal.

We got down to work right away. Ms. Lee read us a newspaper article about how these kids and their teachers set up a group to work together on solving problems at their school. They were called Problem Solvers (PS). We got lots of great information from the article. Then we used our word processor to create a guide for our school. So here it is.

# The Rosewell Avenue
# Problem Solvers Guide

*Presented by Ms. Lee's Class*

## Introduction

This program is set up to help students learn to get along and solve their own problems. It is designed for the senior grades, 4, 5, and 6, and is to be used only by highly trained Problem Solvers.

**Step I:** *Early Training.* Get a teacher in your school to go into the grade 4, 5, and 6 classrooms and teach the students some basic problem-solving skills. These might include:

1. Be an active listener. Learn to really listen to what people are saying. Play some games that involve listening skills, such as repeating a whispered message around a circle.

2. Use "I" messages to communicate. Take responsibility for your own words and feelings. Role playing is one way to help you learn to express your feelings.

3. Learn to read body language. People use their bodies as well as words to communicate. For example, standing with your arms crossed over your chest might be a way of saying, "I don't want to communicate."

4. Use eye contact. Practise looking into peoples' eyes when you're trying to talk to them. Viewing a film about how to stop conflicts in the schoolyard might help too.

**Step II:** *Elections.* All students who are interested in problem solving can run in an election. Two problem solvers will be elected from each grade 4, 5, and 6 class. Everyone gets two votes. One vote can be for yourself, but your second vote must be for someone else you think would make a good problem solver. When voting, remember to consider these points:

1. Will the people you vote for be responsible and do their duties well?
2. Would you want them as partners on yard duty?
3. Would you want them to solve problems for you?

**Step III:** *Leadership Training.* The winners of the election will be given more training on how to handle problems. They will meet once a week for training and to get to know each other. There will be three weeks of training and then they will be ready to be Problem Solvers.

**Step IV:** *The Uniform.* Each PS must wear a special shirt while on duty. This helps the kids in the yard to know who the Problem Solvers on duty are. The Rosewell shirt will be bright yellow and have the words Problem Solver printed on them in big blue letters. The shirts have to be large enough to fit over a coat.

**Step V:** *On Duty.* The Problem Solvers should be on duty during morning and afternoon recess. They will need to leave class a few minutes before recess to put on their shirts and meet with their partners. Each PS works with one partner in the schoolyard. They patrol the yard looking for any problems that may be happening, and wait for students to come to them with problems.

**Step VI:** *Solving a Problem*. A student will come to the PS with a problem. For example, Van might say, "Albert is shouting at me." The PS team would then go over to Albert and ask if he and Van would like help in solving their problem. The kids with the problem can choose to speak with the PS team or with a teacher. If they won't accept help from either, they have to go to the Office. The Problem Solvers must have the kids agree to abide by the following points:

1. Work to solve the problem.
2. Tell the truth.
3. Don't interrupt while the other person is talking.
4. Don't call each other names.

**Step VII:** *Weekly Meeting*. A meeting will be held once a week for the PS and their teachers to discuss any problems they may have had in the schoolyard. **Special Note:** Any type of violence is to be reported to a teacher immediately. PS teams are not to get involved in such situations.

If both kids agree to the conditions, each person is interviewed by the PS team about what happened. The PS then ask the students to try to come up with a solution to their problem. They may also give advice about solving the problem. Once a solution has been found, the following terms must be agreed to:

1. Both students must accept the solution.
2. They have to apologize to each other.
3. They agree formally that their problem has been solved.

**Well, that's our report, and Principal MacKay loved it. In fact, Rosewell started the program shortly after we presented our Problem Solvers Guide. And guess who were elected as Problem Solvers for our class? Me and Pui-Ying Chiu.**

# My Grandma

*by Letty Cottin Pogrebin*
*Illustrated by Leanne Franson*

I used to be ashamed of my Grandma.

I know that's a terrible thing to say, but it was true until last Wednesday, so I have to admit it.

My Grandma lives in our basement.

She moved in about a year ago after Grandpa died. Mom and Dad put a Chinese screen in front of the water heater and stuck a blue rug on the floor, so it looks pretty nice for a basement. Grandma says she can be happy anywhere as long as she has a hard bed and her exercise bike.

My Grandma loves her exercise bike. She rides for twenty minutes every day and she's almost seventy. She makes me ride for ten minutes because she says I'm only half as strong as she is even if I'm sixty years younger.

"A sound mind needs a sound body," she says. But she talks funny so it comes out *a zound mind nids a zound body.*

My Grandma is from the Old Country. When I was little, I thought that was just a nice way of saying she was *old*, but it means she wasn't born here. She grew up speaking Yiddish and Polish and Hungarian and I forget what else, but whatever it was, it definitely makes her English sound weird. That's just *one* of the things I used to get embarrassed about.

At first I was glad she moved in because she's kind of fun to be with. She lets me braid her long grey hair, and she teaches me things like gin rummy and knitting and how to make those little pastries with nuts and sugar rolled up in them. She calls them *rugalach*. I can't say it as well as she does so I call them ruggies.

I used to love Grandma's stories, too.

No matter what we're doing, she always slaps her forehead and says "Oy, that reminds me of a story."

One time when we were baking, she remembered how she once churned butter so long it turned to cheese. "I was daytime dreaming," she said with a laugh.

And once we were sewing and my scissors wouldn't cut, and she told me about this guy who used to ride through the streets of her town with a special cart with a sharpener.

"He made a clang on his cowbell," she said, "and we ran out from our houses with our dull knives and scissors, and he sharpened them on a big stone wheel. Such sparks you never saw."

I told her that sounded pretty neat. I wish we had one of those guys in our neighborhood.

When there's a full moon outside, my Grandma always pulls down the window shades near my bed. She says it's bad luck if the moon shines on you when you sleep. I make fun of her superstitions but she always says, "You never know . . . you never know."

Mostly, my Grandma's stories are funny. But sometimes they're scary—so scary that I have to scrunch up my shoulders to cover my ears, even if I've heard them before.

For instance, there's the one about her aunt and uncle who lived in this poor little town with a winding brook and a wooden bridge. It sounds like she's starting a fairy tale, but I know she's working up to the part about the pogroms. That's when these soldiers called Cossacks attacked and burned Jewish people's houses. We're Jewish.

"If it wasn't for the pogroms," she says, "a lot of Jews who ran away to North America would have stayed in Europe. Then they would have been killed by the Nazis. So maybe the pogroms were a blessing in disguise."

To me that's like saying, "Good thing we were hit by a two-tonne bus or we might've been flattened by a ten-tonne truck."

But to Grandma it's a happy ending. Grandma *loves* happy endings.

The trouble started when my friend Katy found Grandma's false teeth floating in a glass on the bathroom sink. I guess I was so used to seeing them that I didn't even notice them anymore. But Katy noticed. She shouted, "Yuuuck! Gross!" and started laughing hysterically, and pretending to talk to them and making them talk back. I had to get down on my knees and *beg* her to shut up so my grandmother wouldn't hear and get her feelings hurt.

After that happened, I started to realize there were a *million* things about Grandma that were embarrassing. Like the way she grabs my face in her palms and murmurs *"Shaine maidel,"* which means "beautiful girl" in Yiddish. What would Katy say if she saw *that*!

Or how Grandma always says her *B'rachas* before she eats. *B'rachas* are Hebrew blessings that thank God for things. All I

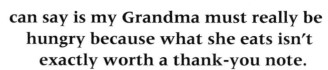

can say is my Grandma must really be hungry because what she eats isn't exactly worth a thank-you note. Chopped herring is gross enough but white bread soaking in warm milk could make a regular person throw up.

And that's just the problem. My friends are regular people. So when Katy or Jill or Angie are around, I have to worry about what Grandma's going to do next. Once she took me and Jill out to Burger King, even though she doesn't eat there herself because they don't have kosher meat. Instead of ordering our hamburgers well done, she told the person behind the counter "They'll have two Whoppers well-to-do." Jill burst out laughing, but I almost died.

Another thing I spend half my life explaining is why Grandma wears a wig. It's not a designer wig either. It's like the hair on an old doll, sort of frizzy and brownish.

I have to explain that she doesn't wear it because her hair fell out and she doesn't wear it to change her hairdo. She wears it because the Jewish law she believes in says that after a woman gets married, she's not allowed to show her own hair to anyone but her husband.

"But he died," Katy said. "So what does he care now?"

Some things you just can't explain.

After a while, I started wishing I could hide my Grandma in a closet. It got so bad I even complained to my parents.

"You guys are at work all afternoon! You don't know what it's *like*. She barges in and talks non-stop. She tries to teach us thousand-year-old games that aren't even in English. And she looks like the Grandmother From Another Planet."

My parents said they understood how I felt, but I had to be careful not to make Grandma feel unwelcome in our house.

"She's had a very tough life," said my Dad.

"Try to make the best of it," said my Mom.

I was trying, *believe* me, I was trying.

Then, like I told you, on Wednesday, something happened that changed everything. My teacher made an announcement that our school was going to be a part of a big Oral History Project. We were supposed to help find interesting old people and interview them about their lives so kids in the future will understand how things used to be.

I was trying to think if I knew anyone interesting when Angie nudged me from across the aisle.

"Volunteer your grandmother!" she whispered.

I was shocked.

"My Grandma??" I said.

"Yeah!" Angie said. "*She's* interesting!"

Interesting? That's the *last* thing I ever thought Angie would say about Grandma!

Well, okay, I said to myself. Why not? Talking is what my Grandma likes to do best. In fact, I've never been able to get her to stop.

So that's how I ended up here. The whole school is in the auditorium for a big assembly and I'm up here on the stage interviewing my own Grandma.

We have microphones clipped to our shirts and TV cameras pointed at us and a bunch of professors are standing off to the side in case I need help asking questions.

Which I don't.

After all this time, nobody knows my Grandma's stories better than I do. I just say the right thing to get her started.

Like when I say "Grandma, why did you leave the Old Country?" she goes right into how the Nazis took over her town.

I've heard all that before. But then she starts telling this incredible story that is brand new to me:

"My parents, they sold all their furniture to buy passage to North America. In the meantime, they hid me in a broken-down barn under a pile of straw.

"Can you believe it?" Grandma says looking right at me. "When I was only a little older than you are now, I was running from the Nazis. Me and my parents and my grandparents got into a big old ship, and people were getting sick during the trip and some of them even died. But we had a happy ending when we saw the Statue of Liberty."

While my Grandma talks, I see all my friends and teachers are listening to her as if she's a great hero. And suddenly I feel so proud of my Grandma, I could burst.

I can hardly wait to ask her the next question.

"How did it feel when you saw the Statue of Liberty, Grandma?"

"Very nice," she says. "When that lady she held up her lamp for us to come in nice and safe, I *knew* everything would be okay. I *knew* it."

Next she talks about her life in North America and I hear her saying something else that she never put in any of her stories before. She's telling us that she loved her family very much, but she has to admit one thing: that she used to be ashamed of her grandmother.

"For twenty years that woman was in this country, but she wouldn't learn English never," says my Grandma about her Grandma. "Such a shame she was to me in front of my girlfriends."

I can't believe my ears. I feel a little stabbing pain in my heart. And right there on the stage I make a *B'racha* to thank God for never letting my Grandma know I was ashamed of her, too.

"Thank you for sharing your experiences—the happy ones and the painful ones," the principal is saying to Grandma. "We're so glad your granddaughter brought you to us today."

Everyone starts clapping really loud. I feel like laughing and crying at the same time. I feel like hugging my Grandma and saying I'm sorry and nominating her for the Grammy Award for Grandmothers.

But I just stand on the stage and listen to the applause, and I feel my Grandma grip my hand tight as we take our bows together.

## ABOUT THE AUTHOR

### LETTY COTTIN POGREBIN

Letty Cottin Pogrebin is a founding editor of *Ms.* magazine and the author of several books for adults. She was also the editor of *Stories for Free Children* and the co-developer with Marlo Thomas of *Free to Be You and Me* and *Free to Be a Family*. She has written articles for many newspapers and magazines ranging from *The New York Times* to *Seventeen* magazine. She has also contributed to many textbooks and anthologies. Letty and her family currently live in New York City.

# Courageous Spirits

*What makes a hero? Here, in their own words, Aboriginal children from across Canada tell you who their heroes are—and why.*

*The Spirit of Haida Gwaii*

## Bill Reid, the Artist

*by Kiel Russ*

**B**ill Reid is the Native hero I want to write about. Bill Reid was born in 1920. He is half Haida. His mom was Haida and his dad was German and Scottish. Bill Reid is a distant relative of Charles Edenshaw, another famous Haida carver. He got to use some of Charles Edenshaw's tools. Bill Reid didn't know he was a Haida until he was in his twenties. That's when he went to see his grandfather, Charles Gladstone, in Skidegate. I think Bill Reid might have felt kind of sad because he didn't really know that he was part Haida until he was older.

I want to be like Bill Reid because he is a great artist. He is one of the most famous carvers in the world. I admire Bill Reid because he became a success even though he had tough times as a kid. He also has Parkinson's disease but he is still trying his best. I always try my best when I play sports and keep on doing it until I get good at it. Then I keep on playing because it is fun.

When I first saw Bill Reid's carving of "The Raven and the First Men," it made me feel I wanted to carve and be an artist. The last major sculpture that Bill Reid carved was called "The Spirit of Haida Gwaii." My Nannie (grandmother), June Russ, and my Chinnie (grandfather), Chief Iljawass from the Queen Charlotte Islands, went to Washington, D.C. to see "The Spirit of Haida Gwaii" be unveiled.

It made me feel proud for them and Bill Reid.

The world needs more people like Bill Reid so they can get back their land, their culture, and do more of the things they used to do—such as speaking their own way. Doing their own kind of carving and making their own rules—rules about where they can log and fish and not to take too many trees or fish.

Bill Reid has made many people respect the Haida culture. He made other people and young Haidas get interested in carving, and I am one. That is why Bill Reid is a hero to me.

• • • • • • • • • • • • • • •

# My Hero, Susan Aglukark

*by Shawna Tatty*

**S**usan Aglukark is the daughter of two famous gospel singers, David and Dorothy Aglukark. She is a very kind-hearted person, and everyone knows that. You could tell by listening to her beautiful voice and that smile on her face.

Susan was born on January 27, 1967, in Churchill, Manitoba. She lived in the Keewatin for most of her young years with her family. She now lives alone in Ottawa and holds a job with the Inuit Tapirisat Council. Her parents live in Arviat. She has four sisters and two brothers.

In an old renovated warehouse, Susan started singing at the age of nine. They fixed up the warehouse and turned it into a small church.

Susan left her family and went on to Yellowknife for high school, since there were no high schools in the far north. Susan had to go for further education. It was all new to her, but yes, she made friends.

She had written about a close friend she once had. Everyone has close friends or had. When she wrote it, it was so good that I wished every young teen could have read it.

Susan's first video was "Searching." Video shots were done in Ottawa and the northern shots were done in Arviat, NWT, a place where she grew up. Three of her relatives are included in the video.

As Susan stated in a couple of

magazine articles I read, she is shy about acting in front of a camera. You would not think so when you see her on video. We sure love to watch the video called "Searching." It was made right for all ages, young and old alike. I found that the best music video and that's when I knew that she was my hero. An Inuk who is able to have that kind of a talent and show us what she's feeling and telling us is so important.

It is good to have different cultures that work with each other. A good example is right here. These are people from different cultures that came together to make a great music video. That goes to show that people can work together to make music and video successful.

Every Inuk should be proud of what she has done. Susan cares for her people, and it shows in the video what our grandparents went through.

She tells young people that we don't have to give up easily on things we have started. I was about to give up on this project I'm working on until I read Susan's words in one of the magazine stories about her: "start something different." It helped me not to give up and work harder at it instead.

Susan dropped out of high school and felt very bad about it, and started something new. She now has her Grade 12 diploma. If we try as hard as she did, maybe we would be able to accomplish what we're aiming for.

Susan is often invited to sing her songs and is enjoyed by all who listen to her sing. It is not always easy for us to start something big. We have to keep trying until we get good at it.

It is important for me to have a hero like Susan that I can write about. I am proud of her. She is a very good example to our people.

## Graham Greene

*by Willow Fiddler*

Graham Greene. He's got to be my hero. My father knows him. He would occasionally come down to Sioux Lookout in Ontario to perform plays for a theatre group. My dad would organize these "after-play" parties and they would get together and have fun. He's gotten bigger since then. The first time I saw him in an actual movie was in *Pow-wow Highway*. That was quite a while ago. Now every movie that opens I see him starring in it. The best I thought was *Dances With Wolves*. There was such a good cast in that movie. Now I see him in *The Last of His Tribe, Clearcut,* and *Thunderheart*.

I myself feel proud of being a Native now because of how much Natives are being noticed and respected by other races. That wasn't always easy.

Graham Greene has a lot of influence on me. I want to become an actress. I think it's important for Natives to try to do their best at what they want and not have others tell them what to do. Other people have had a lot of influence on me too. My parents, friends.

But I've always looked up to Graham Greene. He's the greatest. I'm always telling my dad to take me to Toronto to meet him. What would be really nice is if Graham Greene would come back to Sioux because there are a lot of people who know him and would like to know him. Including me. He will always be my hero.

## Why I'm Proud to be Aboriginal

*by Cheyenne Corcoran*

My mother, Carole Corcoran, is the person I have chosen for my Aboriginal hero. I have chosen my mother because she has had a tough life, but through it all she kept going without quitting. My mother was the first woman elected to our Band Council. She worked hard to make the Band Council give housing to single mothers. She started the first school on our reserve. She had to face many hardships because she was the only woman on the Band Council. She was brave and stood up for what she thought was right. I consider this an act of heroism.

What inspires me about my mother is that she left her family to go to university and got her degree in Law so she could get a good, successful job. I am proud of my mother because she did not quit. My mother was the first person from our family and our Band to get a university degree.

My mother was born in Fort Nelson, BC. She moved to Vancouver in 1985 to go to university. It was important for her to get an education so she could teach her children the importance of education. The hardest thing of all for my mother was when she moved to Vancouver with my sister and me. My dad had to move to the Northwest Territories. We only saw him at Christmas and in the summer. My brother also lived away from us. He lived with his grandparents because they wanted him to stay with them in Fort

Nelson. Three years after my mother started Law school I moved to the Queen Charlotte Islands to live with my dad. He had a job as the school principal there. My mother was in Vancouver by herself until she graduated in 1990.

In October, 1990, the Prime Minister of Canada asked her to work on a special commission on the future of Canada. For eight months she travelled across the country, meeting all kinds of people. It was a very hard job because a lot of people didn't like the Prime Minister and his government. With her busy job she did not have very much time to go home. In 1991 we moved to Prince George. My mother had to go back to Vancouver to take a two and a half month legal course in August. She came home in November, 1991. After that she was an articled law student. She finished her training in July, 1992, and now she is a lawyer.

My mother has received many job offers from the government, First Nations groups, and other law firms. She is not sure where she wants to work next. She would like to help the Aboriginal People get self-government. Self-government is people who control their own actions.

My mother also wants us to have respect and recognition for our Aboriginal heritage when we grow up. My mother has taught me that Aboriginal People have not been treated like Canadians. The governments of Canada have forced most Aboriginal People to live in terrible conditions on Reserves. Aboriginal People have been treated very badly. Until the government realizes this, the Aboriginal People will not have a chance to make better lives for themselves. She says that she will never be proud to be a Canadian citizen until Aboriginal rights are recognized.

The most important thing that my mother has taught me is that no matter how hard things are, you never give up. Even though our family was split up for seven years, when we didn't have very much money or when we had family problems, she never gave up her hopes that she could accomplish her goals.

One special moment that I value in my memory about my mom is when she graduated from Law school. It was a special day. My grandparents, some of my aunts and uncles, my brother, my dad and I were all there to see her graduate. I was proud of my mom and I knew my family was too.

My mother influences me in many ways. She has helped me to see that it is important to get an education and go to university. Most important of all is the way she makes me proud to be an Aboriginal Person and to fight for my rights. I think the world needs more people like my mom because she fights and fights without stopping. She is unique and she gives me a lot of wisdom.

# Not **Ever** Again

by Karleen Bradford
Illustrated by Josée Morin

"Chip! Over here, boy!" Sonia whistled. The golden retriever flashed through the woods like a happy light on this grey February day. The dog raced over to Sonia and gazed up at her with adoring eyes. She tousled his ears and looked back at him with just as much love.

"It's late, boy. Let's go home. We'll take the shortcut." Sonia struck off through the woods.

The pathway cut through the trees, then circled a small lake. The instant Sonia saw the lake she was sorry she had come this way. Last week the lake had been completely frozen. Today, several mallards were swimming in a small, open patch of water out near the middle. Sonia knew the only thing Chip liked better than swimming was swimming after mallards. Chip saw the ducks and he charged.

"Chip! Come! Back, boy, back!"

But there was no stopping him. Chip raced out onto the ice. At the very edge of the open water, he started barking furiously. Suddenly the weak ice gave way, and Chip fell in.

"CHIP!" Sonia screamed.

*Never go out on the ice. Never!* The words had been drilled into her since she was old enough to roam the woods by herself.

What was she going to do now? She was too far away from anyone to go for help. They'd never get back in time.

Chip clawed frantically at the ice, but it kept breaking beneath his front paws. Every time the ice broke, the dog sank under the water. Every time he sank down, he took longer to fight his way back up. Panic overwhelmed him completely. He was drowning, right in front of Sonia's eyes!

Sonia looked at the lake closely. The ice seemed to be fairly solid everywhere except around the open spot. She grabbed a long, sturdy branch and stepped out gingerly.

If Chip had been a person, Sonia could have held out the branch for him to grab. Chip couldn't do that with his paws, but the dog never missed a chance to play tug with sticks or anything else around the house. Maybe he'd bite onto the branch long enough for Sonia to pull him out.

Sonia walked carefully, testing every step. Then she lay flat on her stomach and inched her way closer, holding the branch out in front of her. Now she could see the terror in her dog's eyes. She could hear the strangled gasps as Chip gulped water.

"Stick, boy!" she shouted. "Grab the stick!" But it was no use. Chip ignored the branch completely. He had only one thought in his mind, and that was to get out.

Sonia inched closer. Chip was so near to her outstretched hand! If she could just grasp his collar . . .

Without warning, the ice beneath her gave way. The shock of falling in was so great she didn't even register the near-freezing coldness of it. Unthinkingly, she turned and tried to pull herself back up, but the ice gave way, exactly as it had for Chip.

At that moment Chip scrambled both big paws onto Sonia's

back. Before she knew what was happening, she was underwater with all Chip's weight on top of her. She pushed Chip off with one hand and fought for the surface with the other, kicking as hard as she could. But something was wrong. Something was weighing her down. Her boots! Waterlogged and heavy, they were like anchors dragging her towards the bottom of the lake. No question of kicking them off — they were too tightly laced.

Finally Sonia reached the surface and grabbed wildly for the ice again. Again it broke. Now Sonia realized how heavy her parka was. She took one mitten in her mouth and tore it off, then tried to find the zipper of her parka. She had to get rid of her coat. But her hand was already half-frozen. She couldn't even feel the end of the zipper, much less get it open.

Chip swam around her, no longer panicking now that Sonia was in the water. The huge dog bumped into her constantly. The effort of fending the dog off was so great that Sonia kept going under. Three, four times she went down. Each time she looked up at the clear green underside of the ice. It seemed so far away . . . She had to struggle so hard to reach it . . . She was so tired . . . It would be so easy not to try . . .

*I'm drowning!* With a shock Sonia suddenly realized the truth. *I'm really going to drown!* Suddenly, instead of fear, she was filled with a terrible anger—an anger such as she had never known before in her life.

*I can't drown! I can't drown! I'm too young—I've got too much to do!* The thought of her parents flashed through her mind. How

59

long would it take them to find her? How would they ever believe that she had actually gone out on the ice after all? Then, stupidly—*I haven't even finished my science project!*

The anger was so overpowering that Sonia made another furious attempt to reach the surface. Her hand clasped the edge of the ice. She just held it lightly, letting it help her stay up. For a moment she could almost rest. She looked around her at the empty lake, the darkening woods. There wasn't another person to be seen. Anywhere.

Then, incredibly, she heard a noise and saw a light. Two people on a snowmobile were taking the same shortcut home that she had. With her last remaining bit of strength, Sonia waved her free arm high in the air.

"Help!" she screamed. "Help me!" The noise of the engine drowned out her voice. The snowmobile kept on going.

"Out here!" she screamed again, waving frantically. *Look over here*, she prayed, *look this way!* But with a sickening feeling in the pit of her stomach she realized they didn't hear her.

The snowmobile cut along the edge of the lake, then turned back towards the trees. Just as Sonia saw it disappearing into the woods, the noise cut off. It took Sonia a second to react to the sudden silence. She shouted again. This time one of the riders turned around.

Within moments the two rescuers

flattened themselves onto the ice, one holding onto the ankles of the other. The closest one held out his hands. Fingers touched fingers. Then Sonia felt a firm grasp on her wrists. Slowly, painfully, her body was hauled up and over the edge. She broke into sobs as she felt solid ice underneath her. Another second and they had pulled Chip out, too.

Sonia could barely stand, let alone walk, so one of the rescuers carried her over to the snowmobile. The cold hit her now and she started to shake uncontrollably.

"Sheer luck," one was saying to her. "Sheer luck, kid, that I stopped just then. We'd never have seen you, otherwise."

Sheer luck. Her life had hung by such a thin thread. She looked down at Chip, now frolicking beside her, none the worse for his dip in the icy water. She remembered the outrage, the anger she had felt within herself. She had almost thrown her whole life away. Her eyes followed Chip. She loved that dog so much. And, undoubtedly, she had saved Chip's life by going out onto the ice.

But would she do it again?

There was only one answer now.

"No, Chip," she whispered under her breath.

"Not again. Not ever again."

## ABOUT THE AUTHOR    KARLEEN BRADFORD

Karleen Bradford was born in Toronto and grew up in Toronto and Argentina. She's been writing as long as she can remember. She was always scribbling as a child and would even convince unwilling friends to act out the plays she was writing. She attended the University of Toronto where she earned her Bachelor of Arts degree in languages. Her husband is a foreign service officer with the Canadian government. Because of this, she has spent many years travelling to various countries with their three children and their pets. As she says, "Each of the different countries I've lived in... has given me ideas for stories." Karleen and her family currently live in Owen Sound, Ontario.

## How to Solve a Conflict

One day there was a boy named Jon and another boy named Mark. Both of them got into an argument and asked the teacher what to do. The teacher said nothing and Jon tried to remember what to do if you got into an argument. Jon thought hard for a while about how to solve a problem and remembered about the five steps to solve a conflict. Number one is to listen to both sides and what they have to say. Number two is do not argue, just listen. Number three is tell the truth. Number four is to say you're sorry, and the last one is to shake hands. So Jon and Mark did those five things and they eventually became friends once more. The next day there was a girl named Kathrine and a boy named Adam and they got into an argument. When Mark heard them arguing, he yelled out "use the five steps to solve a problem!" They thought about it and followed the rules and they didn't argue with each other again. So now every time someone gets into an argument they use the five steps to solve a problem. The End.

— Stephen Cadieux, Age 12

I sometimes like writing when I'm bored, usually about sports and horror stories. I never knew that I was going to be picked. I was very surprised about it. I guess I should start writing a bit more and maybe I could become a pretty good writer.

Stephen Cadieux

I wrote this poem because I care about my classmates, my teacher, and my family. I would like it if everyone was friends.

Deidre Berry

## What Friendship Is . . . .

Friendship is a relation that can't be broken.
Friendship is a person that can be trusted.
Friendship is a person that will be there for you and won't let you down.
Friendship is a person that will be responsible and will help you if you're hurt.
Friendship means that you will share and care for one another.
Friendship means that someone will be there for you and will help you learn from your mistakes.
That's what friendship is.

— Deidre Berry, Age 10

# Free the Children!

In April, 1995, a twelve-year-old boy named Craig Kielburger read an article about the murder of Iqbal Masih, a Pakistani boy who had campaigned against child labor. Craig decided he had to do something. With some of his classmates, he founded Free the Children, an organization dedicated to fighting child labor. But that was just the beginning of the story. . . .

Canadian Press

Craig Kielburger addresses a group of journalists and supporters after arriving at Toronto's Pearson International Airport.

Winnipeg Free Press, November 27, 1995

## Boy's plea launches fight to free his peers
### Help stop child labor, 12-year-old urges unions

By Michele Landsberg
Canadian Press

TORONTO — Roar after roar of applause greeted the speaker standing at the microphone before 2000 trade union delegates.

At last, after a fractious week of deliberation, the working women and men of the Ontario Federation of Labor had found a speaker and an issue to ignite them.

"India has 50 million child workers and 55 million unemployed adults. Every child at work means an adult out of work," declared Craig Kielburger.

"Child labor is keeping the Third World poor. Factory owners prefer to hire children because they are cheap labor, easily intimidated, and won't organize trade unions to fight for better working conditions."

If Craig's call against child labor was electrifying, it's partly because he is only 12 years old.

Delegates, flushed with enthusiasm, rushed to the microphones as the standing ovation for Craig slowly faded.

"My local is so moved by the dedication of this young brother, we pledge $5000 to his campaign," boomed the first speaker.

Forty minutes later, a staggering total of $150 000 had been pledged.

The Globe and Mail, January 22, 1996

# Youngsters' child-labor plea upstages PM

## Canada should be setting an example for other countries, Thornhill boy says

**BY JOHN STACKHOUSE**
*The Globe and Mail*

NEW DELHI — Amidst the Canadian stampede to sign big business deals this week in India, Craig Kielburger and Asmita Satyarthi pulled off an Indo-Canadian agreement that did not make the starting lineup for the visiting trade mission.

The two school children issued a joint declaration to eradicate child labor.

"We ask that both countries help in the elimination of child labor and the exploitation of children," said the declaration signed yesterday in New Delhi by Craig, 13, and Asmita, 10.

While praising the trade mission for trying to renew economic and political ties between Canada and India, Craig said it was missing a human face.

"What must be given equal importance is the issue of human rights, especially child labor and bonded labor, and the exploitation of children," he said. "These are issues which must be raised."

Craig's visit was co-ordinated by the South Asian Coalition on Child Servitude, a New Delhi-based organization that works to free children from bondage and rehabilitate them into society. Asmita is the daughter of the coalition's founder, Kailash Satyarthi.

Craig launched his own organization, Free the Children, last year when he heard reports about the murder of a boy working in a Pakistani carpet loom.

He began his seven-week children's crusade last month, travelling to Bangladesh, Thailand, Nepal, and now India. He plans to visit Pakistan and southern India before returning to school in Thornhill, north of Toronto, in late January.

Montreal Gazette, February 17, 1996

# Canadian schoolboy takes up struggle against child labor

IAN MacLEOD
*Ottawa Citizen*

Thornhill, ON — Craig Kielburger, 13, has a soft face and a sharp mind. Words and facts and figures about child labor pour out of him in his choirboy's voice. His hands punctuate his rapid-fire thoughts with the thrust of a finger here, the chop and swoop of a hand there.

"These children couldn't go to school because there were no schools. Exploitation must be stopped. Consumers have to ask questions. It simply comes down to a question of political will," said Craig, who returned late last month from a one-boy tour to protest the use of child labor in Southeast Asia. He met Mother Teresa in Calcutta, won over the world press in New Delhi, and upstaged Prime Minister Jean Chrétien in Islamabad, Pakistan, by forcing him to address the issue during his Asian trade mission.

By the time his plane touched down in Toronto, Craig's seven-week trip had turned into a human-rights crusade that captured the attention of Canadians.

He explains the complexities. Simply not hiring child workers won't work. There has to be meaningful employment for their parents, better wages and working conditions. Countries like Canada have to persuade exporters not to use child labor, or they will face stiff, escalating fines.

(TOM HANSON/Canadian Press)

Craig Kielburger, a 13-year-old Ontario boy, talks to a 10-year-old street vendor in New Delhi yesterday after helping to upstage the Canadian trade mission in India by making a plea to end child labor.

*Calgary Herald, February 22, 1996*

# Advocate rejects advisory post

AGNES BONGERS
*Southam Newspapers*
OTTAWA

Children's rights advocate Craig Kielburger is politely declining an offer to become a special adviser to Foreign Affairs Minister Lloyd Axworthy to avoid compromising the integrity of his cause.

"Free the Children will always remain an independent group representing children and youth," Kielburger said Wednesday.

"We will not directly affiliate ourselves with any political party (or) the government

### NO POLITICAL CONNECTION

"We have and will continue to support these groups, but this support must come with no strings attached."

Axworthy invited Kielburger to Ottawa this week.

The Grade 8 student said he was asked to become an advisor on children's issues but he doesn't want any political party to cash in on his newly found fame.

The teenager gained international attention when he upstaged a Canadian trade mission to Asia by making an impassioned plea to end child labor in countries such as India and Pakistan.

It earned him the attention of Prime Minister Jean Chrétien who met him personally.

It also earned him the visit to Canada's capital, where he's gained the ear of some MPs and the Canadian International Development Agency.

### NATIONAL FAME

Talking comfortably to reporters, the poised Kielburger at times spoke like a seasoned politician, at other times a naive idealist.

He went to Asia to examine the hardship of child laborers, travelling on his mom and dad's tab.

His fledgling Free the Children has gained national fame through speaking engagements funded by garage sales and sales from soft-drink stands.

*The Vancouver Sun, March 5, 1996*

# Crusader against child labor tells students in Surrey they can make a difference too

Craig Kielburger said when he heard about the suffering of Pakistani carpet worker Iqbal Masih he could either watch it on the news or do something.

GERRY BELLETT
*Vancouver Sun*

Put Craig Kielburger with 500 other kids in the school gym and he's invisible. At least until he opens his mouth.

That's when this 13-year-old international crusader against child slavery stands out.

In only a few months this Toronto teenager—founder of Free the Children—has upstaged Prime Minister Jean Chrétien, met Mother Teresa, been wooed by the Canadian government, and done more than anyone else to raise the national consciousness on the evils of child slavery.

On Monday he brought his campaign to Surrey's Elgin Park secondary school and left the students and faculty emotionally dazed by it all.

Kielburger is a natural orator with the stage presence of a matador—fearless, without qualms and ready for anything.

Someone asked if he was afraid of being dismissed as a young idealist. Not a bit.

"If that's the case then we need more idealism in the world today," he said.

"Young people dream high so they can reach higher—they can do more."

Last April when Kielburger was 12 years old he read a newspaper story of Iqbal Masih who escaped from a Pakistani carpet factory. The boy had been enslaved since he was four, ran away at the age of 10, told his story to the media, then was shot to death.

"I was the same age and I looked at my life and I looked at his and I realized how lucky I was. I realized too that someone has to speak out for these children."

He spoke with some of his school pals and they decided that "we could either sit back and watch it all fly by on the news or do something."

The group formed Free the Children, raised some money, and Kielburger's parents paid his airfare to Asia, where he started his tour in Bangkok last December.

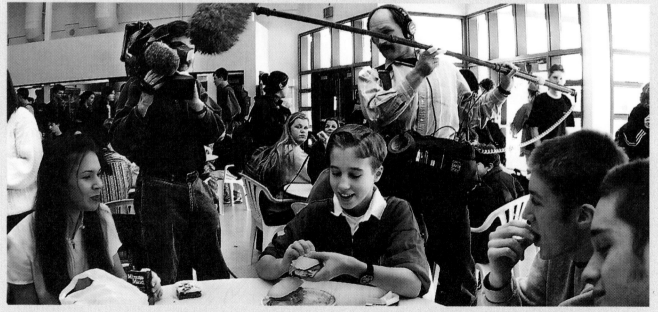

IN THE MEDIA EYE: Thirteen-year-old Craig Kielburger (centre) joins some students at Elgin Park secondary school for lunch Monday as a crew from the CBS television newsmagazine *60 Minutes* films him for a segment on his work as a crusader against child slavery.

*Calgary Herald, May 3, 1996*

# Canadian kid wins U.S. fans

ROBERT RUSSO
*The Canadian Press*
WASHINGTON

Just when you think he can't be real, that he's too poised, too polished for a 13-year-old, Craig Kielburger acts his age.

"I got one of his napkins," he says in wide-eyed wonderment after a visit to the home of Vice-President Al Gore.

"You know what it says on it? It says Vice-President of the United States. He has his own napkins!"

The high-pitched giggle and the brief diversion from his constant crusading on behalf of exploited child workers is almost a relief.

He is a kid. But he's not your usual head-banging, roller-blading rebellious teen.

"He was very polite but very direct in his conversations with my husband and he got my husband's attention," Tipper Gore, wife of the vice-president, said in a brief interview.

While his fellow Grade 8 students in Toronto were hitting the books, Kielburger was pushing the hot-buttons on the political and network talk show circuit in Washington. It was Asia in February, a congressional committee in Washington last week, New York next week, and Haiti later this summer.

Research for his speeches is faxed to him at the offices of volunteers who lodge and feed him.

Kielburger has been a sensation in the United States since CBS's *60 Minutes* did an unyieldingly flattering profile of him and his Free the Children organization on April 21.

---

*The Halifax Chronicle-Herald, September 7, 1996*

# 'Made from suffering of children'

## Kids' advocate tells heartbreaking tales

by Mary Ellen MacIntyre
Cape Breton Bureau

SYDNEY—When a roomful of 12-year-olds sits quietly, you have to wonder why.

Almost 60 children sat mesmerized Thursday night at the Delta Inn here, listening to a boy who was just a year older than they.

All chattering, laughing, and roughhousing ceased as the words of internationally known child advocate Craig Kielburger began to hit home.

The Thornhill, ON, boy told them stories that seemed to break their hearts—unbelievable stories about children just like them, some older, some much younger, all exploited and all abused.

"One girl who I'll never forget was only eight years old and she wore a ribbon in her hair," Craig said.

"She worked at a recycling plant in India, separating hypodermic needles that came from hospitals and from the streets. She wore no gloves, not even any shoes, in fact we saw her step on a hypodermic needle in her haste to get her work done.

"She simply did not know the dangers. She had never heard of things like AIDS."

Craig said he had to keep his conversation with the girl brief or else her master would have beaten her for being away from her work too long.

The children's faces reflected their horror at what they were hearing. They exchanged looks of incredulity. One young girl held a hand over her eyes during one particularly descriptive portion of his speech.

This was the inaugural meeting of Youth Speaks Up, an organization of local Grade 6 students designed to help the children prepare for the changes coming up next year in junior high school. It emphasizes helping the students understand the evils of violence, drugs, alcohol, smoking, peer pressure, and racism.

Craig was the group's first guest speaker. A clean-cut boy whose command of the English language belies his age, he heads up Free the Children, an organization he formed in 1995 to help exploited and enslaved children of the world.

The Vancouver Sun, October 2, 1996

# Teen crusader urges children's protector

## A Toronto boy famous for fighting child labor in the Third World wants a national ombudsman

**JACQUIE MILLER**
*Southam Newspapers*

OTTAWA—A Toronto boy who is famous for his crusade against child labor in the Third World turned his earnest gaze to problems at home Tuesday.

Craig Kielburger and four young supporters from Ottawa arrived on Parliament Hill to ask for a national ombudsman for children's rights.

They talked about poverty, homelessness, deadbeat fathers, and parents who beat their kids. The five children took turns speaking before microphones they could barely reach, occasionally tripping over big words.

But press conferences are nothing new for Keilburger. His campaign against child labor has captured worldwide attention.

The 13-year-old spoke without notes, his polished delivery punctuated with statistics, gestures, and rhetorical flourishes.

"I don't have to travel to India, to Brazil, or to Pakistan, to see the suffering of children," Kielburger said. "Canada is a rich country. Why is it that one in five Canadian children live in poverty?"

Kielburger also called for parenting classes in high schools, more co-ordination between children's aid societies, and an end to government spending cuts that hurt children.

"Today we are here to tell the politicians that we are not the ones who spent Canada into debt, we are not the ones who should be punished," he said.

---

The Globe and Mail, January 29, 1996

# Child-labor activist adamant about living up to obligations

## Thornhill pupil coming home to deluge of demands

BY MICHAEL GRANGE
The Globe and Mail

TORONTO—When Craig Kielburger returns tomorrow from his seven-week tour of southeast Asia, there will be more waiting for him than a few friends and family.

Ever since the 13-year-old child-labor activist made headlines across Canada and news around the world this month by demanding that Prime Minister Jean Chrétien move human rights—particularly the fate of child laborers—higher on his agenda during an Asian trade mission, requests for the Grade 8 pupil's time have kept his parents'

telephone ringing and fax machine churning.

There have been more than 50 interview requests—and counting. Australia's Channel 7 wants to send a film crew to do a documentary. The ABC network in the United States is sending a film crew from New York; freelance writers from all over North America want to tell Craig's story; school groups, service clubs, and business organizations from Montreal to Vancouver are inviting him to speak.

"We are inundated," his mother, Theresa, said. The special-education teacher and her husband, Fred, a high-school

*Craig Kielburger, of Free the Children, addresses a news conference on Parliament Hill in Ottawa.*

French teacher, have seen their backstage roles expand from that of chauffeurs and sponsors (they paid for Craig's flight) to travel agents and media-relations agents. She said they are being careful about who does the interviews and when they are to be held.

# At the Avenue Eatery

*by Gayle Pearson*
*Illustrated by Margot Thompson*

Lindsey scanned the menu at the Avenue Eatery. Every so often her father took her out to dinner alone. They'd been to some good places, like Betty's Ocean View Diner, Soul Brother's Kitchen, and Little Joe's for spaghetti. The Avenue Eatery was the place they came to most often. It was close by and the pies were fifteen centimetres high in the centre.

She readjusted her jacket on the back of her chair so that the zipper was not digging into her back. Then she picked up the menu again. She might order a burger, fries, a salad, and dessert because she'd had soccer practice and was awfully hungry. Plus, she liked to order red meat when her mother wasn't along. Her mom often said, "If it's red and dead it's not to be fed."

Every time the door opened, the wind gusted across the room, making the little yellow flames shiver inside their red candle holders. Lindsey wished it would snow. It seemed cold enough. She remembered it snowing once when she was back in the fifth grade, and school was cancelled for the day.

Magnolia, the server, flashed them a warm, lingering smile. Then she came by to wipe down the table.

"Hi, you two." Magnolia stood right over them, and she gave Lindsey's father a smile and winked.

Jeff, her father, blushed when he said, "Hey there, Magnolia," so cool-like back to her.

"I guess we need another minute," said Jeff. "I think the kid here is still undecided."

"Sure enough, hon." Magnolia slipped the ticket into her uniform pocket and waltzed away to another table.

Lindsey leaned across the table. "Dad, she called you 'hon.'" Her father had on his teal blue sweater and it brought out the blue in his eyes. She understood why a woman would call him "hon."

"Oh," said Jeff, shrugging. "I think she said 'hum.'"

"Hum? You think she said 'Sure enough, *hum*?' Right, Dad." She laughed.

"Well, don't tell your mother. Okay?" He winked at her over the top of his menu.

"Mm mmm."

"No, I mean it. Be sure not to tell your mom."

"Oh, all right."

"No, *really*, no matter *what*, don't tell your mother!" He winked again and grinned.

"Oh, Dad. You're goofy," she laughed.

She didn't always get along with him. He had a strong streak of obstinacy. Last week, for example, they were shopping for ingredients for a mocha bundt cake. He said the recipe called for whole wheat flour only and she said she was sure the recipe said half whole wheat and

half unbleached white flour. He bought whole wheat. He was wrong. He made it with all whole wheat anyway. The cake weighed about sixteen tonnes after baking. Each bite sank to the pit of their stomachs like a large stone. He didn't give up. He said it was delicious and ate it until he was sick.

Magnolia whizzed by with two platters of chicken and french fries. Lindsey liked Magnolia and hoped she had someone at home who would wait on her.

Cold sandwiches, hot sandwiches, dinner entrees with salad and potatoes. . . . She cupped her hands over the red candle holder to warm them. Magnolia brought her father some coffee.

"Great. Thanks," he said, and laid down his menu.    Jammed into one

of the booths against the wall, a crowd of teenage girls screeched and chattered. Everything seemed hilarious to them. Though Lindsey enjoyed going out with her dad, she couldn't wait to be old enough to do that herself. If I'd gone shopping with Lorry and her mother, Lindsey thought, we might have stopped for pizza. These choices were sometimes hard to make. She would have gone with them if she hadn't gone out with her dad. Her mother hated shopping so they only went when it was absolutely necessary, and by her mother's standards those times were rare. She didn't much like it herself. She'd never be one of the "mall dolls."

Her father was dumping NutraSweet into his coffee. She should bring up something interesting to talk about, but it wasn't always so easy. Sometimes you had to give them a topic or they just sat there, dumping NutraSweet into their coffee, and stirring, stirring, stirring. Surely the coffee was all stirred up by now. I mean, it's not *cement*, she said to herself. She wondered if most fathers were like that, say in places like Florida and Alaska, France and China. He could tell a good story on paper, though. She had to admit that. Almost any evening she could pick up the *Tribune* and read a story with his byline.

"So what'll it be, Linny? You won't have to pass a quiz on the menu."

"Very funny, Father." She fingered the menu's tattered edge, suddenly feeling dizzy with hunger. Everyone around them was eating. Ketchup drizzled down a little boy's chin at the next table. His mother twirled pasta around a fork and his baby sister blew an arc of peas across the table.

Lindsey glanced again at the table of girls, where hilarity still reigned. Every single one had her hand on a burger or french fry. "A burger," she said aloud, "and . . ." She was about to say "salad," because she felt the presence of her mother somewhere close to her left shoulder. But she turned to her right and said "fries" instead.

"Burger it is," said Jeff.

At that moment Lindsey spied a solitary figure stuck away at a corner table just off to the right. Her stomach did a little flip-flop. She did not like to see people eating alone. It made her feel sad, blue.

"I wish Magnolia would hurry," she said. "I'm starved."

"Well, I guess she's pretty busy. I'll try to catch her eye, though."

She didn't want to be caught staring, so she raised her menu a little higher and peered over it at the lone woman. The woman raised the spoon to her lips and blew on it. She put the spoon down and pushed up the sleeves of a heavy dark coat.

"It's a funny way to get someone's attention," said her father, clearing his throat.

"What?"

"To say that you 'catch someone's eye.' You know, like she was just walking by, I stuck out my hand, and bingo!"

Lindsey smiled. "Dad, you have a sick sense of humor."

"Here she comes. Let's be ready so we don't seem like nit-brains."

Lindsey tried to get a better look at the woman alone. Her coat seemed shabby. Her grey hair looked as though it hadn't been combed. Lindsey had a sudden

horrible thought, that that could be her mom someday, or her dad. Now she didn't feel hungry at all.

"Maybe I'll just have some tea," she said with a sigh.

"Tea? *Tea*?" Her father looked puzzled and surprised. "I thought you were hungry. What's the matter?"

"I—I was hungry."

"So?"

Lindsey shrugged. "I guess I'm not as hungry as I was. Dad, it just

bothers me to see someone eating alone like that." She nodded in the woman's direction.

Jeff turned to look over his shoulder. He scratched the back of his neck and drew his eyebrows together. "Gee, I didn't know she was here. That's Mrs. Glass."

"You know her?"

"Su-u-ure." He sipped from his water glass, taking his time. "I'm surprised to see her here alone. Really surprised."

"Yeah? Why?" She watched the woman break a cracker in two and drop it into her bowl.

"Well, she usually looks like a barnacle, thirty-four grandchildren clinging to her arms and legs. Get the picture? She lives with one of her daughters not far from the lake in a house that's not very big. I doubt she has much privacy."

Lindsey studied her father's face. He knew a lot of people from the newspaper. They were always bumping into someone he'd written about—a pet psychologist, a woman who'd had a lung transplant, a man who'd written a book about the art of flirting. . . .

"I'll bet she doesn't have her own room," continued Jeff. "Bet she shares a bed with one of those grandkids, and the kid's still in diapers and when she wakes up in the morning she's lying on a big wet spot."

Lindsey laughed. "Oh, Father, you don't really know her."

"O-o-oh, yes," he insisted,

stretching and yawning. "I don't remember the exact story. Maybe she was the one who won the half-marathon in the senior division last month."

"She doesn't look like a runner to me."

"You've got a point there. I don't remember that coat in the photo. But I wouldn't worry about her, Lindsey, she's getting a well-deserved rest. When she eats at home, the kids drool on her spaghetti. Now what's happened to Magnolia? I've got to concentrate on catching that eye."

Lindsey pulled a wisp of hair away from her face and smiled at her father. She knew he loved her a lot and didn't want her to feel bad about anything.

When she looked at the woman alone now she saw an entirely different person, someone enjoying the luxury of time to herself. Her coat was ragged from being pulled on by so many kids. Her hair was messy because she was so busy combing everyone else's. She was only eating a bowl of soup because she loved soup and none of her grandchildren would eat it.

"Bingo," said Jeff.

Magnolia retrieved a pencil and pad from her uniform pocket.

"I'll have turkey on rye, no mustard. Lindsey, you want a burger?"

Lindsey was about to say yes when she noticed the table where the high school girls had been sitting. It was littered with plates smeared with ketchup and bits of food.

"A banana walnut waffle and a cream soda without ice."

"Very creative," said Magnolia. She made a few marks on her pad and hurried away.

Lindsey mused over the fact that her father almost always ordered turkey sandwiches, breaking his routine with tuna or chicken. His tastes were plain. She liked that. She liked that he wasn't the type of person who wanted to impress people by ordering steaks and fancy wines. She didn't know why she liked that, but she did. She hoped when he finished the sculpture he was working on at home, it would make him famous, even if he didn't care about things like that.

". . . starved," her dad was saying, drumming his fingers on the table.

As Lindsey twisted her bracelet around and around her wrist, she spied another person alone, a man sitting at a small table near the centre of the room. She had not seen him come in. He was a homely sort of person, with a long thin neck and a small head fringed with grey hair, and she hoped that wasn't why he was eating alone. He picked at a salad, absorbed in a paperback book.

"Here, hons." Magnolia set the two plates down on the table. Lindsey looked at the man and then down at her waffle, piled high with sliced bananas, chopped walnuts, and a dab of whipped cream.

"Empire State Building," said her dad. He scraped excess mayonnaise off a slice of rye bread.

The syrup smelled rich and sweet, but she was not sure she could eat it. "Right," she replied. She broke off a piece of the waffle with her fork and then made a face. She couldn't seem to help it.

"What's wrong, Lindsey?"

She detected just the slightest hint of impatience in his tone of voice. "Hmm? I don't know, Dad. Maybe I'm coming down with something. I'm just not that hungry after all." She would try to eat, she knew she'd be hungry later on if she didn't, but her stomach had lurched once again at the sight of the old man alone.

Her father studied her for a moment. Then he said, "Well, perhaps you should've ordered something easier on the stomach, soup or some salad, like Art over there." He nodded in the homely man's direction.

Lindsey sighed. She sliced a piece of banana in half and ate it, then a small bit of waffle. She did not look over at the man. "Art?" she repeated. "Don't tell me you know him too?"

"Well, I don't really know him. But someone that I know knows him. She was just saying that she'd heard that Art's wife was out of town visiting relatives and he'd been pretty lonely."

"Oh," said Lindsey. So she was right this time. She kept her head down and tried to focus on her food.

Her dad hurried on. "So my friend said that Art's wife just called him, yesterday I think, just to tell

him how much she missed him, and that she was coming home a few days early. I bet that he was so happy he decided to take himself out to dinner, and he looks like he's really enjoying it, doesn't he?"

Lindsey gave in to her curiosity and lifted her head. Art turned a page, sipping coffee or tea. She supposed you could be happy in a quiet sort of way, even if you were alone. You didn't have to be jumping up and down or near delirious with laughter, like the crowd of girls, to be happy.

"Think you can handle that waffle or what?" asked her dad.

"Oh, I'm doing all right," she said. "It's good. Want some?"

The wind battered a cold sheet of rain into their faces as they emerged from the Avenue Eatery. They hurried huddled together down Telegraph Avenue, passing an old woman crouched in an alcove, half buried under a pile of filthy rags. A grey kitten slept curled up on her lap. Lindsey gaped at the woman as they passed and then turned her face up to her father's.

"Dad . . ." she said.

He clutched her hand and squeezed it, but he didn't say a word.

## ABOUT THE AUTHOR
### GAYLE PEARSON

Gayle Pearson was born and raised in Chicago, Illinois. She now lives in the San Francisco Bay Area. She has written several books for children including the award-winning *Fish Friday*. Gayle says that "Writing fiction is an exciting occupation.... I never know what I'll discover when I embark upon a new book, what I'll find when a character leads me into an abandoned building, for example, or how she will feel about what she finds there." Gayle is currently at work on her sixth book.

# Windows

## In Nola's World

by Wasela Hiyate
Illustrated by Stephen Taylor

Nola watches from the television set
"windows to the world"
She calls it
witnessing the gunshot wounds
laughing at soap operas
why leave the house?
what's there to see?
there's Africa, America
and Europe on TV
But the volume is too low to hear
the distant crying of a child
the dying words of a soldier
In this domain
the anger of millions is drowned
by the rattling of sewing machines
in a factory
by the knowledge that lunchtime at McDonald's
begins at 10:30.

# Yonge and Dundas

*by Kim Berg*
*Illustrated by June Lawrason*

As I walk across the street
at the corner of Yonge and Dundas,
I see a little old man,
sitting by the newspaper stand,
watching the people go by,
but talking to no one.

I walk farther down
and see a man
playing a harmonica,
begging for money.

Looking in the windows of the Eaton Centre,
I feel lonely and tired.
I decide to walk back,
back to where I came from,
back to the corner of Yonge and Dundas.

# Downtown

*by Juliet Jackson*

The streets are full of people.

Their eyes are fixed as far as
They can see BEYOND each other,

Towards the concrete horizon, definite,
Tall against the dark velvet sky,
Stopping vision visibly.

The streets are full of people,
Sadly smiling, emptied of desire,
And going nowhere.

## The Letter

Thrauque worked at a jeans factory in Thailand. It was a hard job, and she only got three pennies a day, but she couldn't let her family go hungry. Thrauque sighed and lay down for a second.

The supervisor was a shrewd man with a greedy look in his eyes. One of his workers, a young woman, was lying in the dirt. The supervisor grinned and went after her. Meanwhile, a letter was flying through the air. It was put on a truck in Bangkok and was driven out to the jeans plantation a few miles out of the city.

The Letter Carrier hopped out of the truck and sprinted across the cotton fields to the supervisor, who was about to yell at Thrauque. "Letter for you, sir." The young Thai looked uncomfortable. The supervisor grunted and opened the letter.

Dear Jeans company,

I am in Grade Four and we are learning about developing countries. Can you please be nice to your workers?

Thanks,

Paula Wilson

The supervisor sneered and threw the letter on the ground, but Thrauque picked it up. It had saved her.

— Ashley Waring, age 11

I've never really been in to writing before. In fact, I was never really good in writing. Then, out of nowhere, I just seemed to become more creative and actually enjoyed writing. Now that my work is actually in a book, I think I'll keep on writing.

Justin Toribio

## My Perfect World

I have a world where everyone is treated equally. There is no racism, and there is no sexism. I have a world where someone can walk the street at 11:00 at night and say "How do you do?" to a stranger without fear. I have a world where there are no weapons or fighting. I have a world where there are no poor people and no rich people. I have a world where there's no need for lawyers and we can all forgive each other with a hardy handshake. I have a dream of a Perfect World.

– Justin Toribio, Age 13